The LOST ART _of_ TRUE BEAUTY

LESLIE LUDY

HARVEST HOUSE PUBLISHERS
EUGENE, OREGON

Published in association with Loyal Arts Literary Agency, LoyalArts.com.

Cover by Left Coast Design, Portland, Oregon

Cover photo © James Pauls/iStockphoto

THE LOST ART OF TRUE BEAUTY
Copyright © 2010 by Winston and Brooks, Inc.
Published by Harvest House Publishers
Eugene, Oregon 97402
www.harvesthousepublishers.com

Library of Congress Cataloging-in-Publication Data
Ludy, Leslie.
The lost art of true beauty / Leslie Ludy.
    p. cm.
ISBN 978-0-7369-2290-6 (pbk.)
ISBN 978-0-7369-3710-8 (eBook)
1. Christian women—Religious life.   2. Beauty, Personal—Religious aspects—Christianity.
I. Title.
BV4527.L83 2010
248.8'43—dc22
                                            2009021250

Printed in the United States of America

18 19 20 21 22 /VP-NI/ 11 10 9 8 7

CONTENTS

How beautiful are the arms which have embraced Christ, the hands which have touched Christ, the eyes which have gazed upon Christ, the lips which have spoken with Christ, the feet which have followed Christ. How beautiful are the hands which have worked the works of Christ, the feet which treading in His footsteps have gone about doing good, the lips which have spread abroad His Name, the lives which have been counted loss for Him.

—Christina Rosetti

AUTHOR'S NOTE

*O*ver the past decade I've had the privilege of interacting with thousands of Christian young women. Every so often I meet a young woman who is truly a cut above the rest; a girl who has forsaken the empty beauty promoted by the culture and embraced a heavenly radiance that impacts everyone she meets. Each time I encounter such a young woman, I'm reminded of Song of Solomon 2:2: "Like a lily among thorns, so is my darling among the maidens" (NASB). And I am inspired afresh to pursue the stunning beauty of Christ rather than the fleeting beauty of this world.

It is my hope and prayer that this book will inspire you toward the same end. We live in a world where hollow feminine allure is applauded and where true feminine radiance is mocked. I hope that as you read these pages you will catch a vision for feminine beauty as God intended it to be. No matter what your version of feminine beauty has been up to this point, it's never too late to let Christ transform you from the inside out with *His* version of loveliness; the kind of beauty that reflects His glory and impacts others for eternity. He is eager and willing to shape us into lilies among the thorns.

Here are a few things to keep in mind as you read. This book is filled with practical advice on applying Christlike feminine beauty and grace to our daily lives, addressing issues such as social etiquette, dressing with dignity, and communicating with Christlike grace. But, as the first few chapters of this book will explain, it is imperative that these practical principles flow out of the right foundation, a life that has been overtaken by Jesus Christ and a heart that is fully and completely His. If we try to exude feminine dignity and grace in our own strength, we will only achieve a humanly manufactured beauty that will not reflect the glory of God. So I encourage you to put the practical advice offered here in its proper context—a heart full of love and gratitude to our King and an inner life transformed by *His* grace.

Some of the principles in this book may seem a bit old fashioned. Honor, decorum, ladylike dignity—these are not ideas promoted by modern society. To many of us, they are foreign concepts. That's why this book is called *The Lost Art of True Beauty.* If you choose to let Christ overtake your femininity, you will exude a beauty that is altogether strange to the world around you. And yet it is this kind of rare beauty that has the potential to make an eternal difference in this world.

In this book I share several examples of the specific ways God is teaching me true Christlike feminine beauty. However, these examples are not meant to imply that I'm a finished product in this arena. I am continually being stretched and challenged in these areas, and I know God will be continually refining me into His likeness for the rest of my existence on this earth. I also use examples of many young women I've observed up close. Some reflect heavenly beauty, and some reflect the counterfeit beauty of the culture. In all of these cases the names and some details have been altered in order to protect privacy.

I attempt to write all of my books in a casual, down-to-earth style—as if you and I were sitting across from each other in a coffee shop and having a heart-to-heart chat. I hope you will feel that way as you read this book. This is a topic that is very close to my heart. I know God has a tremendous plan for your life and your femininity, and I pray that this message will encourage you to become fully and completely His.

THE VISION

Exploring God's Pattern for Feminine Loveliness

*How beautiful and how delightful you
are, my love, with all your charms!*

Song of Solomon 7:6 nasb

About a year ago, my husband, Eric, and I visited Disneyland with our kids. Hudson, our three-year-old, found great delight in the It's a Small World boat excursion, which we dutifully rode 12 times. Harper, our one-year-old, clapped and giggled with wild enthusiasm during the parades and developed a special bond with a life-sized Eeyore, who remains her very favorite animated character. We had an unforgettable time. I had never been to Disneyland before and was impressed by how fairytale-ish everything was.

While in the Magic Kingdom, it seemed that every few minutes another little girl would walk by in a princess costume. Each time the girl would have a happy smile on her face and walk with her head held high. Sometimes she would do a little spin just to watch her frilly dress swish around. She was living out the ultimate little-girl fantasy—to be a real princess in an enchanted fairy tale, even if just for one day. I almost wished I were eight again.

When I was a little girl, I loved wearing frilly, lacey, puffed-sleeved princess dresses—the more poof, the better. But back then the Disney Princess outfits hadn't come onto the scene, so I had to settle for wearing fancy nightgowns or bridesmaid dresses my mom picked up at second-hand stores for my "dress up" collection. They were always about five sizes too large, but I loved wearing them anyway. I would twirl around the backyard and pretend I was the most beautiful princess in all the land.

Nearly every woman I've ever met has at one point in her life imagined that she was a beautiful princess, twirling gracefully in yards of satin and silk, with gallant noblemen fighting duels in order to win her hand in marriage. And judging by the hundreds of little princesses walking around at Disneyland, this is a dream that continues to thrive within the hearts of little girls everywhere.

Princess merchandise is wildly popular among little girls today. Outfits that make you look like a princess; movies that showcase beautiful princesses; and even princess nightgowns so you and your friends can have a princess pajama party. For some reason, the idea of becoming a princess seems to capture the intrinsic longing in every girl's heart to be fully feminine—to glow with grace, radiance, and loveliness.

It's an innocent desire. In fact, I believe it's a God-given desire. But as we progress from childhood into young womanhood, the culture quickly warps and twists our longing for feminine beauty into something altogether different than the Disney Princess version.

I can't remember exactly when it happened to me. What had started as a fun game of imagination eventually morphed into a desperate longing to somehow become beautiful and desirable. But the older I grew, the more discouraged I became in my pursuit of beauty.

When I was 14, I joined a modeling school. It was one of those places that promised to turn you into a goddess in just six weeks. The fact that I had braces, glasses, frizzy hair, shockingly pale skin, and bushy eyebrows supposedly did not matter; nor did the fact that I was gangly, awkward, and utterly style challenged. I was assured that the amazing instructors and makeup artists at this world-class institution could transform even the ugliest duckling into the most glamorous swan. So week after week I showed up, learning how to apply bronzer to the top of my cheekbones, how to tame my wild hair into a silky-smooth texture, and how to walk with my neck high and my hips forward (just in case I was ever recruited to strut down the runways of Paris.) I was even taught how to do a mock TV commercial for Maybelline, looking flirtatiously into the camera and coyly unveiling my amazing beauty secret to the world—a brand-new volumizing mascara.

I'm not really sure why my parents agreed to this ridiculousness— and even paid for the classes, no less. I think it had something to do with the fact that they felt sorry for me. For years I had been mercilessly teased about my appearance every day at school. I was desperately insecure. It always seemed as though other girls achieved effortless beauty, while I struggled and strived but never got there. Most of my friends had beautiful olive skin with year-round tans, salon-perfect blond hair that never went flat, and of-the-moment clothes straight out of a Guess catalog. I, on the other hand, was plagued with ghostly pale skin, frizzy brown hair, hopelessly crooked teeth (and thus three miserable years of braces), and a disturbing ineptness at making my outfits look even remotely trendy. At that point in my life, I had never been described by the opposite sex as "hot" or "pretty." The most I could hope for was that guys would label me as "nice" and want to be friends with me, but a large majority of them used me as verbal target practice. They could sense my insecurity and found great delight in pouncing on it.

I still remember walking home from school one May afternoon, my skinny legs revealing my glowing white skin beneath a knee-length skirt. A carload of high school boys drove by, and one of them yelled mockingly, "Get a tan!" I was deeply mortified. (I will spare you the story of my subsequent attempt at using self-tanning cream, which ended up making me look strangely akin to one of the orange Oompa-Lumpas from *Willie Wonka and the Chocolate Factory*.)

It had been easy enough to feel like a princess when I was eight, twirling around the backyard in a frilly dress, but the older I became, and the more of the real world I experienced, the more I began to feel like an ugly stepsister instead of Cinderella.

It didn't matter that my parents had repeatedly told me, "You are beautiful just the way you are!" My youth leader's lesson on "Accepting your own inner beauty and getting comfortable in your own skin" had not helped. And my school counselor's lectures on the importance of self-esteem hadn't made even the slightest difference in my life. The bottom line was that I wanted to be beautiful, not with some vague "inner beauty" that had no value in the real world, but with the kind of sexy, alluring, culture-pleasing appeal I saw on billboards and TV. Somewhere between playing with my frilly dress up clothes and doing the fake Maybelline commercial shoot, I had become convinced that this was the one road to true happiness and the only way to find real love.

I'm not sure if modeling school made any real difference in my physical allure. I certainly did not look like a model by the end of it. One thing I do know—I spent nearly every waking moment of my life for about two years trying to make myself more appealing to the culture and to the opposite sex.

Eventually, all of my efforts did achieve a measure of outward beauty, and I finally began to gain guys' attention. But the ironic thing was that I still felt hopelessly ugly. The first time a guy asked me out, I thought he was joking and started to laugh. And when another guy told me I was pretty, I was shocked. I looked at him in confusion and then blurted, "Really?"

For all the time I spent chasing after the culture's beauty standard, I never seemed to actually get there. Sure, I might have graduated out of my frizzy-haired, pale skin, gangly-and-awkward phase. But no matter how much makeup I put on, I still didn't look like one of the models on the cover of *Seventeen* or *Vogue*. No matter how much I deprived myself of fries and milkshakes, my thighs never seemed to get as skinny as the girl on the Abercrombie poster. And no matter how many guys showed interest in me, there were always scores of other girls who received far more male approval than I did.

My search for feminine beauty, marred and tainted by modern society, had led me to an existence entirely centered upon myself. Instead of pursuing the elegance and nobility that my fictional childhood heroines exuded, I was pursuing the sensual standard of pop culture. Instead of twirling around in a flowing princess dress, I was sauntering down the halls in skintight designer jeans and push-up bras. There wasn't anything graceful or feminine about it. It was all based on sex. The sexier you were, the more beautiful you were.

It was anything but a fairy tale, and I was anything but a princess. In all of the fairy tales I'd grown up with, the heroine might have been beautiful, but she was not admired for her sex appeal. Rather, she was admired for her poise, grace, gentleness, courage, and feminine charm. (And, by the way, the idea of graceful, heroic femininity didn't originate in fairy tales—they are part of God's perfect design for a woman. We'll talk more about this later on.)

When I was young, I had spent hours imagining I was a captivatingly lovely heroine, exuding a sweetness and charm that caused even the birds to come rest upon my finger as I walked through the forest. When I saw injustice, I would quickly rush to offer help and protection. And when confronted with evil, I would sacrifice my own personal happiness to protect what was right. I used to dream about meeting a gallant prince who would be fascinated by all the amazing qualities he saw in me; a man who would slay dragons and conquer kingdoms in order to win me for his own.

But by the time I was 14, I had come to the sad realization that modern guys couldn't care less about feminine grace or nobility. They measured your worth based on the size of your chest and the shape of your body. They measured your desirability based on how quickly they could get you into bed.

Modern culture scorned fairy-tale femininity. Nearly every magazine cover or fashion ad portrayed the same image of "beauty"—a haughty-looking young woman with an icy scowl on her face, waifish clothes draping her anemic body, and her lifeless eyes lacquered with ghoulish black liner. This, apparently, was the standard for womanly allure—the type of girl that guys were attracted to and that society applauded.

So I traded in my pursuit of true feminine beauty for the cheap counterfeit presented by the culture. The result was a season of hellish misery; throwing myself at guy after guy, only to be used and carelessly discarded; tossing all dignity and modesty to the wind and flaunting my body everywhere I went; exchanging wholesome conversation for profanity and crudeness; ignoring the needs of others and adopting an attitude of selfishness and rebellion; filling my mind and heart with the perverted images of Hollywood and the media. Of course, because I was a Christian, I put limits on how far I let these things go in my life. I always made sure I was a step or two ahead of my secular peers when it came to morality, but that didn't keep me from being steeped in compromise.

From the world's perspective, I was on the right track to becoming a desirable young woman; a woman who had forsaken the archaic, restrictive, old-fashioned ideas about feminine modesty and dignity and embraced the empowerment of a self-focused, sensual existence. But a couple of years into this pattern, I finally recognized how empty my life was. I had male attention—but it only led to one broken heart after another. I had a measure of sensual beauty—but it only made me feel like a sex object. I had social status and popularity—but it made me feel fake and shallow. I had parties and entertainment—but they made me feel slimed and dirty.

It was right around that time that I encountered a young woman in her twenties who was altogether different than any modern young woman I'd ever seen. Her name was Kristina. She was a missionary.

She was the most radiant girl I'd ever met. Her face literally glowed. She was beautiful—but it was not a contrived beauty, propped up by outward things like clothes and makeup. Rather, her beauty seemed to emanate from somewhere within her. Her eyes sparkled with passion. Her smile lit up an entire room. She was entirely others focused and seemed to completely lose sight of herself. Most men groomed by modern culture wouldn't have given her a second look. She didn't carry herself with the seductive, flirtatious air that guys always seemed to respond to. She didn't dress to show off her figure. In fact, she didn't pursue guys at all. She was far too busy living out a passionate romance with Jesus Christ to be pining after an earthly prince.

She did not possess worldly allure, but she had something far better: a radiant loveliness that reminded me of the princesses in my childhood fairy tales. It was obvious that her beauty was the real thing—and it far surpassed the hollow counterfeit I'd been chasing after for so many years. I was awed and inspired by what I saw.

Suddenly, all I wanted was to be a little girl again—carefree and innocent, floating in my frilly princess dress and pretending to be a fairy-tale heroine. The souped-up sensuality and shallow self-focused femininity I had pursued in recent years had brought nothing but heartache. When I pondered how far I'd strayed from true feminine beauty, I felt heavy with regret. Was it even possible now to return to those days of childhood innocence? Could my femininity ever be restored after I had spent years throwing it to the wind?

That night I knelt beside my bed with tears of remorse streaming down my cheeks. "God, forgive me!" I cried. "I have strayed so far from You. I have chased after empty, worldly things for so long. All the while I've been proclaiming to be a Christian, I've been living for myself. Forgive me for allowing my femininity to become so twisted. Restore me and shape me into the kind of girl You designed me to be. Cleanse me from the filth of the world and make me new."

Though I had distanced myself from God for two years, that night I felt His presence like never before. I knew He heard my prayer. And

I felt a gentle assurance in my heart that He had a tremendous plan for my life; something far more fulfilling than the path I'd been pursuing. But first He needed my life.

He was asking me for absolute surrender; to lay down all of the things I'd been clinging to for security. Over the next few weeks, I began to lay everything on the altar—my desire for male attention, my craving to always have a guy in my life, my addiction to social status and popularity, my need to always have the latest clothes and read the newest magazines...the list went on and on. I knew this was not supposed to be a theoretical decision. Many practical and often painful decisions had to be made in order to build my life around Jesus Christ rather than the pleasures of the world.

I began saying no to the frenzied social activities that had been the center of my life and helped me climb the popularity ladder. I started avoiding the usual hookup spots that had allowed me to be noticed by potential romantic flings. I relinquished my obsession with beauty and clothes, and I decided to spend my energies pursuing a deeper relationship with Jesus Christ rather than pouring all of my effort into trying to look a certain way. I threw away stacks of shallow magazines and tossed out clothes that had been purchased for no other purpose than to show off my body in a sensual way.

I made the difficult choice to walk completely away from the dating scene, and I determined I would not get into a romantic relationship until God had showed me he was to be my future husband. Until then, my focus was on Jesus Christ, not on pursuing the opposite sex.

These were certainly not easy commitments to make. But, thankfully, I did not have to make them alone. Jesus stood tenderly by my side, giving me strength to obey and whispering assurance and peace to my heart. I didn't know what the future held, but I knew I was right with Him. He finally had first place in my life. He was now in control, not me. And for the first time in years, I felt happy and fulfilled.

During the next season of my life, my femininity was completely transformed. My understanding of beauty was radically altered. God didn't merely restore my childhood innocence and return me to the days of dressing up like a princess. Rather, He gave me a breathtaking vision for true feminine beauty—*His* vision. He taught me the ultimate secret to lasting, spectacular beauty. And it was far beyond the most amazing fairy tale I'd ever imagined.

Danielle is an insecure 21-year-old who struggles with anorexia. "I can't seem to accept myself the way I am," she confessed. "No matter how much weight I lose, whenever I see models on the cover of magazines, those images make me feel fat and ugly. I don't think a guy will ever be attracted to me unless I reach a certain standard. That's why I keep starving myself. I know it's wrong, but I can't help it."

Kayla is a 24-year-old who struggles with a different problem. She is entirely consumed with her outward appearance. "If I'm not wearing something that's completely of-the-moment, I feel distracted and insecure," she admitted. "If I don't have makeup on, I won't even talk to anyone. I spend hours each week improving my wardrobe and style. I know I shouldn't spend so much time focused on how I look, but it seems to be the only way I'll ever meet a guy or get any respect in this world."

Both of these young women profess to know Christ, but they would not be described as radiant, graceful, captivating women who reflect the glory of Jesus Christ. Rather, like the majority of young Christian women today, they would be described as insecure and self-focused.

From eating disorders to self-obsession to extreme dieting to plastic surgery, today's girls are desperately searching for beauty—but they are looking in all the wrong places. Just like my modeling school experience at 14, they are following a faulty pattern, attempting to somehow meet their insatiable longing to be found desirable. The result is the counterfeit feminine beauty we see all around us today, even in Christian circles. Those of us who know Jesus Christ should be the ones showcasing the pattern for true femininity, but instead we are only showcasing the empty pattern of this world. We are battling with the very same insecurities, eating disorders, and selfishness as everyone else.

The Lost Art of True Beauty

When God first began to rebuild my understanding of feminine beauty, my entire outlook and value system had to change. For years I had allowed pop culture to define my understanding of feminine beauty. I had inundated my mind with modern magazines, movies, TV, and the fashion industry—a world that valued the Victoria Secret-model look and attitude. I had been surrounded by peers who applauded self-obsessed, arrogant, sexually aggressive young women. I had tried to venture as close to those standards as possible while still somehow maintaining my Christianity.

Gently and quietly God began to whisper to my heart. "I have a completely different pattern for your feminine beauty, Leslie," He seemed to say. "One that reflects My glory and not the empty charm of this world."

The revelation not only left me feeling excited, but also a bit nervous. Would allowing God to reform my beauty cause me to become drab and ugly? I pictured myself walking around in a dowdy, gray, tentlike dress and with a morose expression on my makeup-less face, my hair pinned in a tight, unattractive bun. The vision made me shudder. Did God have any interest in a young woman being outwardly pretty? Or was He so consumed with inward beauty that He deemed any physical beauty as unhealthy and unspiritual?

Growing up in church, I'd seen every extreme when it came to women and their physical appearance. There was the camp that seemed to think the more glamorous they were, the more impressive they would be as God's messengers to this world. They wore piles of expensive jewelry, caked on layers of makeup, drenched themselves in perfume, dressed in carefully pieced together designer outfits, and kept their fingernails long, pointed, and manicured to perfection.

Then there was the group of women who seemed to think that the less attractive they could make themselves, the more God would approve of them. Either that, or they were so insecure that it seemed they were trying to apologize for their femininity. They hid behind shapeless dresses. They only wore dreary, colorless clothes. They never touched makeup. They kept their hair pinned back or let it hang limply without any kind of style. And, most depressing of all, they never seemed to smile.

Neither example—the showy, glamorous, overdone kind of beauty or the drab, sad, frumpy-is-more-spiritual version—held any appeal to me whatsoever. I'd seen very few examples of women who possessed the genuine grace, poise, elegance, and charm I had longed for in my childhood. And I certainly hadn't seen any inspiring examples of young women my own age.

I had no idea what God's pattern was supposed to look like.

Then I began to read about the amazing, world-altering, Christ-built women of days gone by. I came to realize that though truly beautiful femininity may be scarce these days, it didn't used to be quite so uncommon. Women who exuded enchanting beauty can be found all throughout the pages of Christian history. Like Kristina, they rejected the empty feminine charm of the world and embraced an altogether different kind of beauty—the beauty of Jesus Christ. They showcased femininity as God intended it to be in all its elegance, grace, nobility, and lasting loveliness.

Here are just a handful of inspiring examples.

> A pretty woman, with lovely soft features, kind eyes and dark hair, she was never angry, never impatient, never resentful, she patiently wore away prejudices and hatred by her gentle, gracious presence and her blameless life. She had all the firmness of a man, and yet a more gentle and womanly woman it would be hard to find.[1]
>
> —Said of Lottie Moon,
> young single missionary to China

Her presence lends its warmth and health to all who come

before it; if woman lost us Eden, then such as she alone restore it."[2]

—Said of Lucy Webb Hayes,
First Lady in 1821

She seemed endowed with a peculiar magnetism when you were in her presence so that you could not help thinking yourself in the presence of a being much higher than the ordinary run of humanity. I have heard her pray, and she could offer up the finest petition to the Throne of Grace of any person I ever heard in my life. She was always gentle and kind to the Indians, as she was to everyone else. She took an interest in every one at the mission, especially the children. Everyone loved her, because to see her was to love her.[3]

—Said of Narcissa Whitman,
young married missionary to Native American Indians

They say there is a young lady in New Haven who is beloved of that Great Being who made and rules the world. They say that He fills her mind with exceeding sweet delight, and that she hardly cares for anything except to meditate on Him. If you present all the world to her, with the richest of its treasures, she disregards it. She is unmindful of any pain or affliction. She has a singular purity in her affections. You could not persuade her to compromise her true Love even if you would give her all the world. She possesses a wonderful sweetness, calmness, and kindness to those around her. She will sometimes go about from place to place, singing sweetly. She seems to be always full of joy and pleasure, and no one knows exactly why. She loves to be alone, walking in the fields and groves, and seems to have Someone invisible always conversing with her.[4]

—Written of Sara Edwards
by Jonathon Edwards, her future husband

Can you imagine being described in the way these young women were? Can you imagine glowing with such a divine inner sparkle that everyone who encountered you could not help but be awed, inspired, and captivated? This it what is means to reflect the glory of Jesus Christ through our femininity. It's feminine beauty as God intended it to be. And no matter how impossible it may seem at first glance, it's what each of us are called to.

Sadly, the picture of grace, strength, and beauty painted by these heroes of the faith is light years beyond where most of us are today. Recently I was in a coffee shop, observing a college-aged girl who is known for being an outspoken Christian. She was sitting with one of her guy friends. They were sipping lattes and catching up on life.

The girl is attractive and her personality is outgoing and funny, but there is something about the way she carries herself that is sadly unfeminine. On this particular day, she was speaking and laughing so loudly that everyone in the coffee shop could hear her entire conversation. She was sharing deeply personal things, such as her recent struggle with over-eating and insecurities about her body image. It made me feel awkward listening to her go on and on about herself and her personal struggles with a casual male acquaintance. Nothing appeared to be sacred in her life—her deepest fears and struggles were placed on display not only for her guy friend, but for anyone who happened to be within earshot.

After a few minutes she shifted in her seat and made a crass comment about her backside hurting. She sat haphazardly in her chair, sloppily slurping her coffee, and dangling her legs off her stool in a very unla-dylike way. The more she talked and carried on, her joking became crude, her laughter became obnoxious, and her words became gos-sipy and critical of others. It reminded me of the way I used to behave when I was caught up in the version of femininity applauded by the culture. It's a trap too many of us fall into. The concept of feminine mystique, elegance, and grace is foreign to many of us.

We have become so consumed with trying to make ourselves more appealing to this world; so intent on gaining friends, status, and popularity; and so influenced by the lewdness of pop culture that often the only beauty we are capable of showcasing is a selfish, hollow charm of our own making that will quickly fade with time.

This kind of behavior might seem completely harmless and even normal by today's standards, but it is dismally beneath the version of feminine beauty we are called to exude.

Captivating femininity isn't supposed to only be found in Jane Austen novels or Cinderella stories. Words like *enthralling, enchanting, breathtaking, stunning, delightful,* and *noble* should be the description of every set-apart, Christ-built young woman. It's God's perfect design for each of His royal daughters. Our desire to be a radiant princess didn't originate with Walt Disney—it's a desire placed within us by our Maker. He created us to shine with royal beauty. Not to dazzle with a self-promoting beauty; but to be a sparkling reflection of the stunning beauty of our King. Just take a quick peek at some of the imagery used in Scripture to describe the royal beauty our Lord desires to work within us.

> Listen, O daughter, consider and incline your ear; forget your own people also, and your father's house; so the King will greatly desire your beauty; Because He is your Lord, worship Him…The royal daughter is all glorious within… her clothing is woven with gold (Psalm 45:10-11,13).

> How beautiful and how delightful you are, My love, with all your charms! (Song of Solomon 7:6 NASB).

> Like a lily among thorns, so is my darling among the maidens (Song of Solomon 2:4 NASB).

> Her clothing is fine linen and purple…Strength and honor are her clothing (Proverbs 31:22,25).

> In like manner also, that the women adorn themselves… with good works (1 Timothy 2:9-10).

> And I saw the holy city, the new Jerusalem, coming down

from God out of heaven like a beautiful bride prepared for
her husband (Revelation 21:2 NLT).

When Eric was first attempting to put words to the kind of feminine beauty that set-apart young women are called to, he described it
as a blend between Audrey Hepburn dignity and Amy Carmichael
selflessness. Audrey Hepburn has been called the epitome of elegance
and grace. Though her personal beliefs, Hollywood career, or even
her glamorized physical beauty are not things I necessarily want to
promote, she knew how to carry herself like a true lady—an almost
entirely lost concept among women today. Amy Carmichael is one of
the most heroic women in Christian history. She gave up personal ambi-
tion and pursuits in order to rescue hundreds of endangered children
in India with a devotion that is also a forgotten ideal among modern
femininity. It's the dazzling blend of ladylike grace and selfless devotion that marks a truly set-apart young woman.

When Christ overtakes a woman's life and transforms her from
the inside out, she becomes truly feminine—a picture of elegance,
grace, and loveliness blended with sacrificial selfless devotion to her
King. She becomes a true lady, carrying herself with poise and confidence, yet deflecting all attention away from herself and toward Jesus
Christ. She is enchantingly mysterious, holding her inner life sacred
and guarding her heart with quiet tenacity.

Noble, breathtaking, captivating, Christ-centered femininity is truly
a sight to behold. It's a beauty that does not draw attention to the woman,
but to Jesus Christ. It's a radiance that is not dependent upon age, circumstances, or physical enhancements. It's a loveliness that flows from
deep within—the refreshing beauty of heaven, of a life transformed
from the inside out by Jesus Christ.

Making the Exchange

The first step to discovering true feminine beauty is exchanging all
that we are for all that He is. If we rely on something that *we* possess

to make us beautiful, we cannot receive the supernatural, transforming beauty of Jesus Christ. True beauty is impossible outside of Him. If we obtain a worldly outer beauty, even if we become the most gorgeous, desirable, sought-after model in the world, we only have a propped-up, hollow, fleeting appeal that quickly fades with time and age. Proverbs 31:30 says, "Charm is deceitful and beauty is passing." Have you ever seen a glamorous movie star on the cover of a tabloid once she has become old and lost her beauty? All the appeal and allure she once possessed has faded into oblivion, and the only thing left is what she has on the inside—which, sadly, is not very attractive in most cases.

If we muster all the human heroism and try to become a "good person," we only have a self-made, faltering form of goodness that can never stand against the stunning righteousness of Jesus Christ. Isaiah 64:6 says it perfectly: "We are all like an unclean thing, and all our righteousnesses are like filthy rags; we all fade as a leaf, and our iniquities, like the wind, have taken us away."

Any human beauty, any human value that we might find within ourselves is just a filthy rag compared to the limitless beauty and glory of Jesus Christ. Christ's beauty is perfect. And, in spite of what we deserve, He desires to adorn us with His spectacular glory. It is not *our* unique beauty that must shine for this world to see. It is not *our* own beauty that we must discover and embrace—*it is His.*

C.H. Spurgeon said:

> He is the lily, but His beloved is like He, for He applies His own chosen emblem to her—"As the *lily* among thorns, so is My love among the daughters." Notice that He is the lily and she is *as* the lily—that is to say, He has the beauty and she reflects it! She is comely in His comeliness which He puts upon her. If any soul has any such beauty as is described here, Christ has endowed that beloved soul with all its wealth of charms, for in ourselves we are deformed and defiled!...There is no beauty in any of us but what our Lord has worked in us.[5]

True feminine beauty is not a complicated formula involving hundreds of rules to remember. It's not something that requires spending two years at finishing school or being groomed as a beauty pageant queen. True feminine beauty is the natural by-product of a young woman who has emptied herself, given up her own life, and allowed God's Spirit complete access to every dimension of her inner and outer life.

If you are tired of the counterfeit pattern of the world and ready to discover womanly loveliness as God intended it to be, I invite you to join me as we unearth the lost art of true beauty. No matter how far from feminine beauty you may feel right now, no matter how ugly or worthless you may think you are—this journey is for you. It doesn't matter whether you've struggled with eating disorders, extreme insecurity, weight problems, skin problems, or an obsession with looking a certain way. God has a plan for your beauty, a plan that is beautiful and fulfilling beyond the most amazing fairy tale ever written.

Even now He is gently whispering to you, calling you out of the world's darkness and into His marvelous light. "Listen, O daughter, consider and incline your ear; forget your own people also, and your father's house; so the King will greatly desire your beauty."

Are you ready to respond to His invitation?

SELFLESS BEAUTY

The Captivating Charm of a Gracious Woman

He must increase, but I must decrease.

JOHN 3:30

*If any man will come after me, let him deny
himself, and take up his cross and follow me.*

MATTHEW 16:24 KJV

*A*rianna, a passionate young college student, recently told me
about a new Christian book she had just read. "It was so
amazing," she gushed. "I have finally learned how to love myself and
feel good about who I am!"

Megan, an outgoing 18-year-old, was equally inspired by a speaker
at her church. "She told us we need to be set free from all the wounds
of our past and all the expectations of other people, and just learn to
be true to our *real* selves."

I am continually amazed at how often young Christian women are inundated with messages about the importance of self-esteem. Of course, in Christian circles it may be termed something different— but it's all basically the same package. Whether it's learning to love yourself, learning to get comfortable in your own skin, learning to live to your "true self," or learning to live out your destiny and become a better "you"—messages that promote "feeling good about yourself" are extremely popular in American Christianity.

I grew up hearing messages about self-esteem. In my book *Set-Apart Femininity,* I described a scene from my youth group when I was 14 years old. Our young, hip youth pastor, Kevin Richards, was doing a devotional lesson on self-esteem. He prescribed that we all go home that day, look at our reflection in the mirror, and say aloud, "I love you!" It seemed ridiculous to all of us, and most of us just laughed at his words. But Kevin insisted that self-esteem was actually God's idea. "God wants you to love yourself!" Kevin told us emphatically.

As a young woman growing up in church, I continually heard the message "You are beautiful just the way you are!"

This became an unofficial mantra often chanted to girls in Christian circles, presumably to keep us from ending up with an eating disorder or plastic surgery fetish because we had bought into the world's impossible standards for beauty.

The problem was, no matter how often I heard people say, "You are beautiful the way you are!" I still felt miserably insecure. We live in a culture that lifts up a standard for beauty that is literally impossible to achieve in real life, and I was continually measuring myself against that standard.

Eric and I once talked with a graphic designer who worked for a major clothing label. "In real life, no model looks as perfect as what you see in clothing ads or on catalog covers," he told us. "We digitally alter her photo. We remove several inches from her waist and thighs. We enhance her chest size. We airbrush her skin."

I recently read an interview with a famous Victoria's Secret model who admitted, "Everything about my beauty is fake. From my hair to my nose to my toes—it's all fake."

Our world bombards us with an image of feminine beauty that is not even based upon reality. That standard is what women are told to pursue, and that image is what guys are told to desire.

In Christian circles we are told to appreciate our own unique beauty and accept ourselves for who we are. Meanwhile, we are constantly assaulted by a world that insists we aren't alluring enough—we need to change our bodies, our clothes, and our personality in order to be more appealing. And the same culture that trains young women to become sexy, sultry, and seductive also trains men to lust after women who possess those traits.

The moment we walk out our front door, we see clusters of guys drooling over any skimpily dressed, well-proportioned female who passes by. We watch them lustfully grin at sultry, bikini-clad models on the covers of magazines. We hear them talk about the incredible bodies of the hottest young singers or actresses on TV. We even catch many of them sneaking frequent peeks at Internet porn.

Pretty soon the message "you are beautiful the way you are" falls empty and flat. We are told to love ourselves, but all we feel is worthless and ugly.

Some of us buy in to the pressures all around us, desperately trying to change our bodies, starve ourselves, get plastic surgery, get a makeover, go on a diet—do anything in our power to somehow make ourselves appealing to the opposite sex and to the culture. Others give up completely, tossing the idea of beauty to the wind and becoming sloppy, grungy, and guy-like—letting the whole world know they are sick and tired of the culture's ridiculous standards for women, and that they couldn't care less about being pretty or feminine.

Either way, very few young women escape the culture's relentless agenda with any self-confidence intact. The pressure to meet society's expectations is literally destroying countless young girls' lives.

In her book *A Return to Modesty*, Wendy Shalit described her amazement at how many young women at her college struggled with eating disorders.

> All around me, at the gym and in my classes, I saw stick-like women suffering from anorexia. Who could not feel for them? Or I would hop out to get a bagel at night and see a student I knew—who must have weighed all of 70 pounds—walk into our corner campus hangout, Colonial Pizza. Oh, good, I would think, she's finally going to eat. I would smile and try to give off see-isn't-eating-fun vibes. No, in fact she hadn't come to eat. Instead she mumbled weakly, looking like she was about to faint, "Do you have any Diet Mountain Dew, please? I'm so tired…I have a paper, and I can't stay up because I am so, so tired…" Then in the dining halls I would observe women eating some-times ten times as much as I and then suddenly cutting off our conversation. Suddenly, um, they had to go, sud-denly, um, they couldn't talk anymore. Until that moment I hadn't actually realized that some women really did make themselves throw up after bingeing.[1]

While thousands of young women starve themselves in response to our culture's pressure, scores of others willingly allow themselves to become sex objects.

I've known Lindsey, a 22-two-year old single mom, since she was seven or eight. She was raised in a conservative Christian home and seemed to have a genuine relationship with Christ for most of her life. But when she was 18, things took a downward turn. After a boyfriend broke up with her, she felt intensely insecure and struggled deeply with self-hatred. She started hanging out at bars and clubs, drinking and going home with guys she barely knew. Within months she was preg-nant. But even that didn't alter her course. She kept her baby, but her lifestyle didn't change. Even though she desires to be a good mom to her child, Lindsey's first priority is keeping herself sexually appealing.

Her hair is bleach blond, her eyes are caked with dark mascara, her chest has been surgically enhanced, and her clothes are always skin-tight. The only way she feels any sense of worth or value is when she is with a guy—even if it's just a weekend fling. As a result, she's allowed herself to be used by one guy after the next.

Lindsey represents the plight of countless young women in her generation, desperately seeking self-worth through a Barbie-like figure, a reckless lifestyle, and plenty of male attention. She works hard to exude a carefree attitude, but you can hear an emptiness and hope-lessness in her voice. It's obvious she is miserable, but she doesn't see any other way to survive in our cruel, relentless culture.

With this being the sad state of reality for modern young women, it's no wonder the church has embarked upon a self-esteem crusade. There is no question that today's women are desperately insecure. There is no question that our lives are teetering on the edge of disaster; that self-hatred, self-abuse, and self-destruction have become the norm among the female camp. And, sadly, women in the church are struggling just as much as their non-Christian counterparts.

But is self-esteem the right answer?

Is it true that God wants us to love ourselves and feel good about who we are? Does He long for us to learn to "inhabit our own beauty" or "be true to our real selves"? Is that His goal for His royal daughters? Is that the answer to overcoming our intense insecurity?

I've met loads of Christian young women who have become excited about a message or read a book that "sets them free to become their true selves" and cast off all the insecurities placed upon them by culture, their family, and even the church. But every time, such a message proves to be merely a temporary solution. At first they are just so relieved to hear someone say, "It's time you stopped listening to all this pressure of the world. Don't try to meet other people's expectations. Just be true to yourself!" It's a refreshing message in a day and age where they are bombarded with "you are not good enough" mantras. And it's easy to assume that because the self-esteem message so clearly describes their frustration with the pressures of modern society, it also presents the right solution.

But after a few months, something happens to shake their newly adopted commitment to love themselves. A guy breaks up with them. They are overlooked for a job. Or they simply see too many movies and magazine covers to feel good about themselves anymore.

So once again, they are wallowing in insecurity.

Why doesn't the self-esteem solution provide lasting results? Because the solution presented is all about self. Self-love, self-acceptance, and self-promotion. Love yourself. Be true to yourself. Live to yourself. Some of these messages even go as far as to say that by living this way, you will bring glory to God.

But what is the pattern of Scripture?

Christ said, "Whoever desires to come after Me, let him deny himself, and take up his cross, and follow Me" (Mark 8:34) The word *deny* here literally translates: to forget one's self, lose sight of one's self and one's own interests. We are meant to let all thoughts of self become swallowed up in Him.

Oswald Chambers said,

> It is a tremendous freedom to get rid of all self-consideration and learn to care about only one thing—the relationship between Christ and ourselves.[2]

The secret to becoming the radiant, beautiful princess of our childhood dreams is *forgetting all about our self* and becoming completely consumed with only one thing—*Jesus Christ.* Just as John the Baptist, who declared, "He must increase, but I must decrease."

This isn't just the secret to living out the true Gospel; it's also the secret to glowing with divine loveliness. *It's the cure for female insecurity.*

Think about it. A woman who has truly denied herself, taken up her cross, and become entirely consumed with Jesus Christ is not going to be an insecure young woman, starving herself and obsessed with making herself look more attractive. Rather, she's so enraptured with

Jesus Christ that she's completely lost sight of herself. As Bishop Bardsley put it, "They care not at all what the world thinks of them, because they are entirely taken up with the tremendous realities of their King."[3]

A woman who has yielded her selfish agenda to the Spirit of Jesus Christ, who does not listen to the voice of her self but yields only to the voice of her King, is not going to become a sex object, throwing herself at guy after guy in desperation. Her security comes from a completely different source. She doesn't derive her value from the attention of guys. Her value comes from knowing she has been redeemed and loved by the King of all kings. Her focus is on His desires, not on her own selfish wants.

The women throughout Christian history who have truly glowed with heavenly beauty all had one thing in common—*an emptying of self.* They were so caught up in the things of God that they gave no thought to their own lives. They did not seek to draw eyes to themselves. They sought to bring glory to Jesus Christ alone.

As a result they were some of the most confident, poised, and courageous women who have ever lived. They accomplished amazing things for the kingdom of God. They saved lives. They stood before kings. They rescued dying children. They reformed societies.

And they did it without spending their time and energy focused on self.

Every once in a while I meet a modern young women who is blissfully unaware of herself. Like Kristina, who was so caught up in her love for Jesus Christ and in sharing His love with others that she didn't even notice the pressures and expectations of society. She was completely unaffected by the magazine covers and billboards screaming out an impossible standard for beauty. She didn't even notice the millions of guys lusting after porn stars. These things did not cause her to turn inward and be riddled with insecurity. She wasn't worried about the size of her thighs or if she looked sexy in a swimsuit. She didn't obsess over finding a guy. She was far too busy living out a daily romance with her Lord to notice the empty and meaningless clamor of the world.

The most beautiful women I've ever observed are those who have exchanged a self-focused life for a Christ-focused one. They are confident, but not in themselves. Instead of self-confidence, they radiate Christ-confidence. They aren't spending their time trying to feel better about themselves or inhabiting their own beauty. They aren't even thinking about themselves. Their desire is to decrease so that Jesus Christ would increase.

The secret to overcoming insecurity is not learning to esteem self, but learning to *deny* self.

It may seem backward reasoning at first, but I guarantee if you follow this path, you will discover a freedom you never knew was possible. You will no longer need lectures on feeling better about yourself. You will not need books that remind you how good and valuable and beautiful you really are. Why? Because you will be so swept away by Jesus Christ—the true source of all beauty—that none of those things will seem important. You won't be focused on yourself anymore—you'll be caught up in Him alone and everything else will fade to the background.

Only when self moves out of the way can His spectacular glory come cascading through your life. When Jesus is in His rightful place, all insecurity will fade away and His lasting loveliness will become the mark of your life.

What About Wounds?

I am not trying to oversimplify the issue of insecurity. I realize that many of us have experienced deep wounds and scars. We've been told we were ugly. We've been told we were fat. We've been abused by men. We've been used and dumped by guys. Or we've been chewed up and spit back out by peers at school. Many of us carry around baggage from these experiences, and it affects the way we view ourselves on a daily basis. We are wounded and hurting. Can we experience true healing and freedom simply by forgetting all about ourselves and becoming caught up in Jesus Christ?

The modern church, for the most part, would say it's not quite that simple. It's implied that in order to truly overcome all our hurts, wounds, and fears, we must pour a lot of energy into focusing on our emotional needs, tending to our inner wounds, and being true to ourselves. I remember hearing one young woman talk about some advice a Christian counselor gave her after she had gone through a hurtful experience. "Take some time to pamper yourself," he suggested. "You've been focused on everyone else's needs—now it's time to focus on your own. Buy yourself something you really want. Go to the spa. Eat chocolate. Take time for *you*."

That might sound like appealing advice, but coddling self won't lead to healing from past hurt or freedom from insecurity. Christ said, "Whoever seeks to save his life will lose it, and whoever loses his life will preserve it" (Luke 17:33). If we give up our life—our rights, our agenda, and our whims and desires—in exchange for His life, we will gain everything. But if we preserve, stroke, and indulge self, we will end up with nothing.

Our Lord is not indifferent to the pain we have experienced. He is very interested in healing us and restoring everything that has been stolen from us. He cares more about our wounded heart than even we do. And He has a very simple solution to overcoming hurt and insecurity.

> *Come to Me,* all who are weary and heavy-laden, and I will give you rest (Matthew 11:28 NASB, emphasis added).

When we simply come to Him, not focused on our own problems and issues, but focused instead on His amazing love, power, and grace, He enables us to forget the past and become fully set free to live as a conduit of His glory from this day forward.

As His Word describes,

> Listen, O daughter, consider and incline your ear; *forget your own people also, and your father's house; so the King*

will greatly desire your beauty (Psalm 45:10-11, emphasis added).

One thing I do, forgetting those things which are behind and reaching forward to those things which are ahead (Philippians 3:13).

The process doesn't need to be complicated or introspective. It doesn't require meditating on how we can finally become our true selves. We don't need to think of ways we can pamper ourselves or learn to accept ourselves. We can simply bring our hurts, fears, and insecurities to Jesus, lay them at the foot of His cross, and ask Him to do the rest. As the old hymn goes,

> Turn your eyes upon Jesus,
> Look full in His wonderful face,
> And the things of earth will grow
>   strangely dim,
> In the light of His glory and grace.

If you are carrying wounds and hurts you have never allowed Christ to mend, I would encourage you to take some time in His presence. Write out your struggles, or simply get on your knees and pour out your heart to Him. Ask Him to heal your heart and make you new. If there are people you need to forgive, ask Him for the strength and grace to do that (we'll talk more about forgiveness later on). And then ask Him to turn your focus away from yourself. Once you make the decision to deny self, take up your cross, and follow Him, He will more than supply everything you need to walk this narrow way.

Jackie Pullinger, a missionary in China, tells the story of leading a 50-year-old prostitute to Christ. This woman had been used, abused, mistreated, and defiled in just about every way imaginable her entire life. "How is she ever going experience inner healing?" Jackie wondered. "If we have to talk and pray through every horrible thing she's been through, it's going to take forever." But then the woman began to discover amazing joy by turning outward and helping others in need. She went to hospitals and washed the wounds of the injured. She went to homes for the elderly and brushed the matted hair of the residents. "It was serving others that healed her," Jackie said. This woman who had been so battered, bruised, and wounded chose to deny herself and pour out her life for the cause of Christ. And soon she was made new again. She gained incredible peace, joy, and freedom. She began to sparkle with a beautiful inner glow. She even married a Christian man, and as Jackie said, "She was like a teenager on her wedding day. She had all her life back again."[4] That's God's way. We are restored and renewed as we focus on Him and His priorities and allow Him to turn our focus away from self.

I remember hearing a true story about Eric's grandmother when she was a young woman. Anytime she was going through a time of sadness or inner struggle, she would find someone in her life who was in need—a sick friend, a poor family in the community, or a neglected child—and spend time loving and serving that person. Without fail, her own problems would fade into the background, and she would always find tremendous joy and freedom from turning away from herself and focusing on the needs of someone else. That story has always inspired me. It's helped me realize that the cure for insecurity, depression, and emotional turmoil is simpler than I sometimes think.

The Beauty of Selflessness

Sara is a college sophomore who stands out from among other young women her age. While other girls spend their weekends at parties or the mall, trying to snag a guy or buy up the latest trends, Sara uses her free time differently. Whenever she's not in class or studying, she can be found volunteering at the local nursing home or taking care of needy children in the community. Instead of spending her summer vacation making extra money or going to the beach, Sara spends every break going to the mission field—working in orphanages around the world and ministering to neglected children. She doesn't do any of these things in order to make herself seem more spiritual. Rather, she is passionately in love with Jesus Christ, and she can't help but pour her life out for those in need around her.

When I observe Sara, I notice a radiance, a glow, a loveliness that is unusual in modern young women. It's the beauty of selflessness. Sara has chosen to deny self, to silence the voice of her own whims and wants, and sacrificially pour out her life for Jesus Christ.

In my book *Authentic Beauty*, I described a scene I once witnessed in a college hangout on Friday night. A sandy-haired young woman was spending the evening with her roommate—a severely disabled girl who was confined to a wheelchair. I was amazed at how sensitive and caring the sandy-haired young woman was toward her friend. She seemed delighted to be spending the evening with the girl in the wheelchair, even though they made an unusual pair among the rest of the college students in the coffee shop. She appeared fully content to help her friend with her drink and chat with her about the music, oblivious to the flirting and hooking up going on all around her.

This young woman fascinated me. She seemed to radiate with an unshakable confidence. She could have easily blended in with the dozens of other girls there, but instead she was joyfully pouring herself out to serve her roommate. In fact, she seemed to be having more fun than any other girl in the whole place. As the musician wrapped up his final set, I glanced out the window and saw the sandy-haired young woman whizzing through the parking lot on the back of her friend's wheelchair, the two of them laughing with childlike delight as they raced past rows of cars. From all appearances, this young woman had just had the best night of her life.

Though I never officially met her, I would venture to guess that this young woman knows Jesus Christ in an intimate way. She was blissfully unaware of self—and totally caught up in her King's priorities. It was truly a beautiful sight to behold.

How to Cultivate a Selfless Life

First Peter 4:2 tells us that we should no longer live the rest of our time "in the flesh for the lusts of men, but for the will of God."

Romans 8:1 says, "There is therefore now no condemnation to those who are in Christ Jesus, who do not walk according to the flesh, but according to the Spirit."

First Peter 2:11 exhorts, "Beloved, I beg you as sojourners and pilgrims, abstain from fleshly lusts which war against the soul."

And Galations 5:16 commands us, "Walk in the Spirit, and you will not fulfill the lusts of the flesh."

Throughout Scripture, we are told to yield to the voice of God's Spirit rather than the voice of our flesh. But to most of us, the term *flesh* is just an outdated, vague term we don't really understand.

Here is a vital truth we must recognize in order to live a successful Christian life: *Flesh* is just another word for self—our selfish, put-my-own-wants-first side. Many of us don't even realize we have a selfish, fleshly side. We make decisions based on our own whims and desires. We do what makes *us* feel good. We follow our selfish wants. It's easy to live as a slave to our flesh without even realizing it, especially if we go to church and spend time doing spiritual things.

Our culture, even our Christian culture, has a tendency to encourage us to listen to our fleshly side. *Follow your heart! Pay attention to your emotional and physical needs! Don't just meet everyone else's needs— take time for YOU! What do you want out of life? How can you fulfill your destiny?* All of these questions cause us to focus inward—on what *we* want, what *we* need, and who *we* are.

And yet the Bible makes it clear that if we yield to the flesh, we cannot yield to the Spirit of God. The flesh wars against all the things of God—and it must be silenced in order for us to deny self, take up our cross, and follow our King.

As Ian Thomas so eloquently said,

The Christian life can be explained only in terms of Jesus

Christ, and if your life as a Christian can still be explained in terms of you—your personality, your willpower, your gift, your talent, your money, your courage, your scholarship, your dedication, your sacrifice, or your anything—then although you may have the Christian life, you are not yet living it.[5]

Contrary to what our culture insists, this life is not about us. It's about Christ. And only when we put to silence our selfish side can we radiate with divine heavenly beauty. So how do we learn to yield to the Spirit instead of fulfilling the lusts of the flesh? It starts with simple, everyday decisions.

Often, it starts with your morning alarm clock. Do you yield to the beckoning whisper of Christ's Spirit, asking you to get up and spend time with Him, or do you listen to your own selfish desire to stay in bed? Our entire day is filled with those kinds of decisions. We can either claim this life as our own and do what our flesh desires, or we can deny self, take up our cross, and follow Him. The more we yield to the Spirit, the more we are able, by His supernatural grace, to live the set-apart life He has called us to live.

Daily life is filled with hundreds of choices to either give in to selfish whims or yield to Christ's Spirit. But most of us are so used to obeying the commands of our carnal desires that our ears are deaf to the Spirit of God. Silencing our selfish side takes a lot of focus and a heavy dose of supernatural enabling grace. But Christ is more than interested in equipping us to put to death the desires of our flesh.

When you woke up this morning, did you think of your day as belonging to you or Him? Did you live as if your time and decisions were your own or His? Did you allow the distractions and allurements of this world to turn your head, to occupy your thoughts, or to dictate your choices? Or was He your sole pursuit? How did you spend your free time? Doing what *you* felt like doing? Or pouring out your life for Him?

If you are like most modern young women, you likely have selfish habit patterns that need to be remade by Christ's Spirit. I would encourage you to spend some focused time in prayer and waiting on God, allowing Him to gently reveal those areas of your life that need His transforming touch. Allow His Spirit to open your eyes to any part of your daily existence in which you typically yield to your selfish whims and desires. You may find it helpful to write down anything He brings to mind. Then pray specifically for the grace to silence your selfish side in each of these areas and begin putting it into practice in your everyday life. (For example, choosing to joyfully respond when your alarm clock goes off, instead of lazily pushing the snooze button or angrily hurling the clock across the room.)

It may take a few days, weeks, or months for old habits to fully die, but if you allow God to retrain your daily decisions and enable you to deny yourself, pick up your cross, and follow Him, you will soon understand from firsthand experience what Paul meant when he said, "It is no longer I who live, but Christ lives in me" (Galatians 2:20).

3

THE ART OF SOCIAL GRACE

Showcasing Selfless Beauty in Everyday Life

*Do not merely look out for your own personal
interests, but also for the interests of others.*

PHILIPPIANS 2:4 NASB

The choice between selfishness and selflessness affects just about
every part of our femininity—from what we wear to how we
interact with others. For example, the way we choose to dress and
carry ourselves makes a very loud statement about our inner priorities.
Too many of us have fallen prey to dressing selfishly or seductively.
We want eyes to be on us. We want guys to notice us. Our goal is not
to bring glory to Jesus Christ, but to bring approval and attention to
ourselves. We selfishly lead guys to stumble rather than heroically protecting their inner purity.

The way we act socially speaks volumes about our inner focus. The other night Eric and I were sitting at a dinner we'd been invited to at a family's house. We were served a delicious meal, and the family was fun to be with. But throughout the dinner, the two college-aged sisters held their cell phones under the table and texted back and forth with their friends. They weren't intentionally trying to be rude or dishonoring—but without meaning to, they were giving off signals of "this dinner conversation really isn't that interesting—I'd rather be with my friends right now." It's probably the last thing they meant to imply. They were just unskilled in being sensitive and gracious to those around them.

Many of us don't realize that we are often quite selfish when it comes to the way we act socially in a hundred little areas just like this one. We are typically so caught up in our own world that we don't take time to think about what would be the most honoring to those around us. And as a result, we never showcase the captivating beauty of selflessness that God intended us to have.

Look at the example of Jesus—He always saw the needs around Him. He didn't put his own needs or wants first. His entire life was one of poured-out servanthood and sacrificial love.

Because of His absolute selflessness, He willingly embraced the greatest suffering this world has ever known. Hebrews 12:2 tells us that Christ "*endured* the cross, *despising the shame*" (emphasis added). It was not easy and comfortable for Jesus to give up His life. It was not delightful and pleasant. Taking up His cross caused Him more pain and misery than anyone has ever known or imagined. It was so difficult that the night before it happened He wept exceedingly, sweat drops of blood, and cried out to His Father, "Is there any other way?"

What if Jesus had simply listened to His own selfish wants that night in the Garden of Gethsemane? What if He yielded to what His emotions and human desires were telling Him? What if He had said, "Surely God does not want Me to embrace something that makes Me feel so miserable? Surely I shouldn't see this as an opportunity from My Father! Death is a curse. It's shameful; it's painful. Why would I surrender to something that doesn't make *Me* feel happy?"

In our self-focused culture, it's easy to see absolute selflessness as extreme and unnecessary. A lot of us take the attitude, "I'll just do the bare minimum so I can stay on God's good side"—especially when it comes to dressing modestly, living in purity, and caring for the needs of others. But in light of what Christ did for us on the cross, how can any sacrifice for Him be too extreme? Cultivating selflessness in these areas of our lives is just one small way of reflecting the beauty of our King and expressing our gratitude for what He has done for us.

First Peter 2:21 reminds us, "For to this you were called, because Christ also suffered for us, leaving us an example, that you should follow His steps."

If we want to shine with the stunning beauty of our heroic Lord, we must allow Him to shape every dimension of how we live into His glorious likeness.

Let's explore some of the most practical areas of our femininity in which selflessness can be cultivated.

Becoming Socially Selfless

Once upon a time, nearly every young woman was trained in the art of gracious living. She knew how to exemplify perfect etiquette in every situation. She knew how to dress and carry herself with dignity. She knew how to speak eloquently in conversation. She knew how to excel in hospitality, gift-giving, and community service. She knew how to sit up straight and listen intently when someone spoke to her. She knew how to smile and say hello to strangers. She knew how to stay focused on a task without becoming distracted by a thousand other things.

Before we were married, Eric found a very old book on young women's etiquette. He thought I might find it interesting, so he got it for me. As I read through it, I was intrigued. I had always thought of the old-fashioned etiquette rules that were pushed upon the women of the past as being restrictive, uptight, and snooty, but this book made etiquette actually sound beautiful and refreshing. It was all about how a young woman could let her light shine in this world—how she could use her feminine gifts to bless and serve those around her. The etiquette guidelines were certainly far more extensive than anything expected in our modern times, and yet I found myself almost wishing I could return to a more old-fashioned way of living; a time when people actually treated each other with dignity and respect; a time when young women were refined and gracious in all aspects of their lives.

Today we are so far removed from gracious living that the word *etiquette* is basically nonexistent from our vocabulary and our lifestyles. Somewhere along the way, as the culture became more cavalier toward sin and selfishness, the idea of being dignified, refined, ladylike, gracious, and socially selfless faded into the background. Now young women seem to get far more respect if they are loud, boisterous, rebellious, obnoxious, and sexually aggressive than if they are sweet, polite, graceful, refined, modest, and thoughtful. A popular bumper sticker in the college town where we live says: "Well-behaved women rarely make history." The message being propagated is that in order for a woman to really make any impact upon this world, she must shake off all those restrictive ideas about being polite or considerate and become a pushy, in-your-face promoter of her own agenda.

First Peter 3:4 exhorts women to cultivate "the incorruptible beauty of a gentle and quiet spirit, which is very precious in the sight of God."

God's pattern is the very opposite of the "bad girl" image so applauded in our modern times.

I've heard many Christian women try to downplay the "gentle and quiet spirit" verse, saying that it doesn't really mean we have to be meek and gentle in our personality. One popular book claims that "getting comfortable in your own skin" and "accepting yourself" is what God really meant by having a quiet spirit.

I disagree. I believe this verse means just what it says—that women who adorn themselves with a gentle, gracious, *selfless* attitude are women who shine with the incorruptible beauty of Jesus Christ.

I believe it is possible to have a friendly, outgoing personality and still honor God with a gentle, quiet, selfless spirit. But I've seen many Christ-professing young women who go beyond merely being friendly and bubbly to becoming center stage in every social situation. They are skilled at making sure all eyes are upon them. They are masters at getting guys to pay attention to them. And they overpower anyone who has a more quiet personality, often causing others to be overlooked or ignored. They assume "This is just the way I am; it's the way God made me. I can't help my personality." But their flesh (that selfish, put-me-first side in all of us) has taken control. It's not just their personality; it's their personality being controlled by sin.

Just as it is easy for an outgoing young woman to be controlled by sin and selfishness, a shy, reserved person can fall prey to the very same pattern—it just manifests differently. I've known many naturally quiet girls who draw loads of attention to themselves without saying a word by being sullen, depressed, and inward focused. Because they are so morose, they make everyone around them uncomfortable. They are upset that no one ever seems to reach out to them, but they aren't willing to take the first step and choose to reach out to anyone else. Once again—it's not merely their personality; it's sin overtaking their personality.

When God's Spirit is given His rightful place in a young woman's life, He transforms her personality to reflect His beauty, His grace, His selflessness. He can overtake any kind of personality, whether you are outgoing or more reserved. And either way the end result when He is in control is that *you* decrease so that He might increase. You don't lose your own personality. Rather, your personality becomes what it was intended to be, a tool to draw eyes to Jesus Christ and not yourself.

Very few of us understand how to behave socially in a way that truly brings glory to Jesus Christ and showcases the stunning beauty of our King. I believe it's time that we as young women abandon our self-focused attitudes and return to the good old days when refinement and etiquette were commonplace. Rather than climbing the popularity ladder or playing manipulative social games, let's focus on being gracious, sensitive, and Christlike to those around us. Let's bring true etiquette, true gracious living, back to life. We may not be able to go to finishing school or crochet a doily—but those things are trivial anyway. What matters to Christ is a selfless lifestyle. And when it comes to being socially selfless, there are many practical things we can do, right now, starting today.

Cultivating True Etiquette

It's totally normal today for a young woman to be sloppy and careless in her appearance and attitude; to slouch in her seat, chew with her mouth open, never send a thank-you note, and absentmindedly text with her friends while listening to someone talk. I've even met lots of "Christian" girls who seem to take pride in acting like obnoxious guys—belching, cussing, telling crude jokes, etc. It's almost as if the less feminine they can become, the more hip they think they will be.

Every so often I meet a young woman with poise and grace; a girl who is respectful and refined in every social situation. Whenever I see a young woman with real dignity, I always take notice because such women today are so rare. This summer at one of our retreats, I encountered a young woman who was truly graceful. She dressed with elegance and feminine style. She listened intently when anyone spoke to her. Her words were articulate and thoughtful. She carried herself with poise—she always sat up straight, practiced perfect table manners, and even walked like a lady. She even sent a beautiful thank-you note and gift to me for hosting the retreat. And yet, for all of her polish and refinement, she was not prissy or uptight. She was fun loving, passionate, and hard working, living a life of sacrificial devotion to the least. She painted a wonderful picture of feminine grace and stood out from among other young women as a shining example of Christ's beauty.

Let's go through some of the key principles of etiquette and social grace. As we do, prayerfully ask God's Spirit to speak to you about any that need to be cultivated at a deeper level in your life. It is very possible you already have some or all of these elements of femininity intact.

Even so, it's never a waste of time to revisit the principles of etiquette and continue cultivating them in your life. Because we live in a culture where feminine grace is scarce, and where feminine dignity is openly mocked, it's all too easy to begin comparing ourselves to the dismal standards around us. And soon our own habits can become sloppy without us even realizing it. So think of this as fresh inspiration.

On the other hand, maybe these principles are completely foreign to you. It's possible that the idea of adding etiquette to your life feels awkward and uncomfortable. Ask God to give you strength to move past those emotions, and to fill you with vision and excitement for becoming the graceful woman He created you to be. It's a prayer He loves to answer. Determine in your heart that this is something you are doing to honor and glorify Him and not for the approval or disapproval of other people. And no matter how others respond to the changes in your life, keep your focus on the only opinion that really counts—*His.*

4

EXCELLING IN MANNERS

Social Grace Secret #1

The entire law is summed up in a single command: "Love your neighbor as yourself."

GALATIANS 5:14

Most of us have been taught basic table manners. Don't chew with your mouth open, keep your elbows off the table, don't reach across people to grab things, etc. (If you don't even know the basics, I would encourage you to ask someone in your life who does or read a book on table etiquette.) If you don't already practice the basics of eating politely, start today! Even if those around you display the opposite behavior, remember not to compare yourself to their standards, but the standard of Christ. Paul says, "Whether you eat or drink, or whatever you do, do all for the glory of God" (1 Corinthians 10:31). You won't bring God glory if you display sloppy, disgusting

49

habits while eating the food He has provided for you—you'll only send the message that you are self-focused, ungrateful, and a slave to caveman-like behavior.

What about manners in other situations? I meet a large number of young women who might know how to eat a meal politely, but who are shockingly rude everywhere else. Often, they are rude without even meaning to be, like the two girls who texted with their friends all throughout the dinner party my husband and I attended. I've been around girls who constantly interrupt other people, girls who are loud and obnoxious and overlook the quiet people in the group, girls who act disinterested and distracted when people speak to them, and girls who never express gratitude when someone does something nice for them. I've been around girls who are impatient and demanding toward waitstaff and salespeople, girls who never smile at strangers, and girls who yawn and doze during speeches and sermons.

About a year ago I hosted a small-group Bible study for a handful of college-aged young women, most of whom were involved in ministry leadership positions. Out of the six or seven girls who were there, only one or two of them demonstrated genuine respect for me as I was speaking. The rest of the girls scribbled notes to each other and whispered to the person next to them, acted tired and distracted, checked their phone messages, or got up to leave in the middle of the study without an apology. (Contrary to what this scene might imply, I am not a boring speaker who talks in a monotone!) Again, these young women were not intentionally trying to be rude; they simply didn't realize the insensitivity of their actions. It's dismaying when this kind of behavior is the norm among young female Christian leaders who are supposed to be an example. But they, like the majority of us, have never been groomed in the art of true social grace.

Rude, insensitive behavior showcases not only a lack of manners, but also a lack of respect for other people. Practicing manners is a way of expressing love and consideration for others. Showing honor and respect to those around us is a principle that should translate into every corner of our lives—from servers at restaurants and strangers at the mall to pastors and teachers sharing truth with us and our own family members in the privacy of our homes.

In our book *The First 90 Days of Marriage,* Eric and I write about a lie that many young married couples have fallen prey to—that marriage is the time when you can finally "let it all hang out." There are plenty of jokes about men who burp, scratch, and pack on the pounds and women who stop shaving their legs or wearing makeup once the wedding vows are spoken. And sadly, it is all too true. There is a common assumption that once you have "locked in" your spouse's commitment to you, you no longer need to work to win his or her heart, that you can now be sloppy and careless and throw dignity to the wind. But this attitude shows an incredible lack of respect for your spouse. If a woman only gives attention to how she looks and acts when she goes out into public but not when she is home alone with her husband, it sends the message he is less important to her than a stranger at the mall. If a guy only thinks about being socially polished when he is around others, it shows his wife he doesn't value her as much as his friends. Those most familiar in our lives (family members, spouses, roommates) often take the brunt of our self-focused insensitivity.

How do you make sure you aren't blind to the needs of those around you? The answer is simple. If you are constantly asking yourself the question, how can I be sensitive to those around me and put their needs first in this situation? then chances are high that you are going to naturally be respectful and polite, no matter what the circumstance might be. But if you are only focused on yourself, then most likely you are going to be rude and insensitive without even realizing it.

If manners aren't something you ever give much thought to, or even if your manners just need a bit of polishing, here are a few things you can do, starting today, to begin cultivating respect and sensitivity toward others.

Listen Intently When Others Speak

This is one of the most common blind spots among young women, who are used to multitasking 20 things at a time. You may be used to emailing, texting, or writing notes while carrying on a conversation with someone, but unless you give that person your undivided attention, you send the message that they are not worthy of your complete focus and what they are saying isn't that important. This is also true for public settings, such as church sermons, concerts, or seminars. If you have never spoken on stage before, you might not realize that the person speaking or performing usually notices the people who are yawning, dozing, whispering, or texting far more than the others who are listening intently. I have been a speaker for more than 14 years, and I can tell you from firsthand experience that it is extremely distracting, not to mention disconcerting, to glance out at the crowd and see someone sleeping, talking, or in some other way distracted while I am presenting a message. As a speaker your eye is naturally drawn to the handful of people who are *not* paying attention—those who are fidgeting, yawning, or whispering. They might not mean anything by it, but it still makes the statement, "This message is really boring. I wish I were somewhere else." I can't count the number of times I've been on stage speaking and have had to intentionally choose to ignore those few people who were texting, talking, or sleeping and ask God for the strength to keep delivering my message in spite of the distraction rude behavior was causing me.

Being a speaker and interacting with thousands of people over the years has caused me to become conscious of showing respect when people talk to me. Often after a speaking event, I have a line of young women waiting to ask me a question. And yet, no matter how many people are waiting, and no matter how tired I am, I have learned to tune out all distractions and give my undivided attention to each individual person I'm talking to. Usually, when I take the time to talk and pray with someone, more of a lasting impact is made than anything I might have said from the stage.

Even on airplanes, I make an effort to pay attention when the flight attendants do their required "safety demonstration." I've watched them illustrate how to buckle the seatbelt "low and tight across your lap" and how to put the yellow oxygen mask "over your nose and mouth" numerous times. It's not something I need to see again, but I can only imagine how awkward it must feel to stand in front of a hundred people to present a demonstration when no one is paying the slightest bit of attention. Listening to them talk is just a little way I can show respect.

Take some time to observe your listening habits during daily life. Do you show honor and respect to people who speak to you, or are you constantly multitasking or daydreaming when others speak? As I mentioned earlier, it's often our family members who take the brunt of our self-focused attitudes. Because they are so familiar, we often don't treat them as worthy of the same level of respect we give to others. When family members (or if you are married, your spouse) speak to you, do you look them in the eye and really focus on what they are saying? Or do you type away on your phone or computer and absent-mindedly mumble a response?

If your listening skills need a bit of polish, ask God to make you more sensitive and outward focused. It might even help to make a list of specific situations in which you'd like to become a better listener. Then make a concerted effort to change any bad habits that have formed in the area of your listening skills. It might take some time and practice. If you are like me, you'll have to purposely ignore your inner craving to multitask while people are speaking to you. It might feel awkward and even unnecessary at first. You might be thinking, *I could so easily check my email during this conversation and it would save time later* or *Maybe I should text Jenna during this sermon and see if she wants to meet me after church.* But in those moments ask yourself how *you* would want to be treated if you were the one speaking. If you apply prayer and diligence, you will soon find that you are able to excel in this area. And you will discover the amazing joy of practicing selflessness—even in little ways like this one.

Excel at the Art of Good Conversation

When I was about seven or eight, I didn't know how to carry on a conversation with an adult. Nice grown-ups would attempt to talk with me, and I would stare at the floor and respond to their questions with mumbled, one-word answers. My mom decided it was time for a lesson in "conversation manners." She sat across from me on the bed and held a tennis ball in her hand. "Having a good conversation is like tossing a ball back and forth," she told me. "If I throw the ball to you during a game of catch, it wouldn't be a very fun game if you just caught the ball and held it in your hands. It's only fun if you throw it back to me. The same is true when you are talking to others. When they reach out to you with a question or comment, it's your job to 'throw the ball' back to them by responding with an interesting answer or a question to them."

My mom and I went on to practice having a conversation while tossing a tennis ball back and forth. She would ask me a question like, "How was school today?" and instead of just keeping the ball in my lap and murmuring "Fine," I was supposed to keep the game going by tossing her the ball and saying something like "School was great. We learned how to make snowflakes out of Styrofoam plates. How was *your* day?"

It felt awkward at first, but the tennis ball lesson proved to be very effective in teaching me how to have a respectful conversation with someone and show a genuine interest in others. From a young age, I learned how to respond with interesting answers when people asked me questions, and then to ask *them* questions that showed I cared about their life and not just my own.

Over the past four years I've hosted girls' retreats at my home in Colorado. Young women who desire to learn more about the set-apart life come from around the country, and I've had the privilege of spending time with them on a personal level. For the most part, they are wonderful girls, but it always stands out to me at how few of them are skilled at carrying on a good conversation. It makes me grateful my mom taught me the tennis ball game! Many of us don't know how to keep a conversation flowing effectively, and we make the other person do all the work. When I listen to girls during my retreats, I often notice that they spend the entire conversation either talking only about themselves or answering people's questions with monotone, one-word responses. It is not their intention to create awkwardness. They have just never learned how to be sensitive and others-focused when it comes to conversation.

If this is an area you could use some work in, let me share with you some of the key principles that have most helped me when it comes to the art of good conversation.

Remember Names

When Corrie ten Boom was in a prison labor camp, one of the first things that the Nazis did to dehumanize the prisoners was to strip them of their names. They were called only by numbers. Corrie was referred to merely as "Prisoner 66730" during her entire stay at the camp. Once she was released from prison, simply being called "Corrie" again was an incredible luxury—it made her feel valued and loved.[1]

Remembering someone's name and using it often in conversation is one of the best ways to make someone feel valued and loved. I have to admit, this has become much more of a struggle for me over the past 14 years as Eric and I have traveled to so many places and interacted with so many different people. But I've found that if I simply make an effort to focus on someone's name and file it away in my memory when I first meet them, and then use it early on in my conversation with them—it sticks. It also helps them realize that I truly care about them as an individual. If you really want to brighten someone's day, just smile and say, "Hi, Stacy!" or "How's it going, Mike?" when you pass their way. Even without a lengthy conversation, you send a message that you care about them and that their life has value. Just think about how you feel when someone smiles at you and remembers *your* name.

Use Positive Body Language

When carrying on a conversation with someone, you can send the message that their words have value simply by the nonverbal signals you send. Smiling, nodding, and making eye contact are just a few basic ways to say, "I appreciate what you are saying. It's interesting and important." I can't count the number of conversations I've been in with young women who didn't know how to look me in the eye as we talked. Their eyes darted here and there—and it was all I could do to keep from asking them, "Uh, are you still with me?" Sitting up straight and looking someone in the eye exudes poise, confidence, and interest in the other person. Fidgeting and looking all around the room exudes boredom, insecurity, and lack of value to the other person. (Note: If you disagree with something the other person is saying, you don't want to send off vibes that you are totally on the same page with their opinions. But you can still show honor to their words by looking them in the eye and nodding at the appropriate times to let them know you at least hear and understand what they are trying to express.)

If you turn your back on someone, cross your legs away from them, rest your head in your hand, or slump in your seat while others talk, you give the impression that you don't want to be there. But leaning in slightly when you talk to someone, making eye contact, smiling, and nodding are all physical ways to show you are interested in a conversation.

Ask Insightful Questions

I don't know about you, but I really don't enjoy shallow, trivial conversations. A little bit of small talk is necessary when you are first getting to know someone, but I would much prefer to get to know them at a deeper level than to simply chat about this or that.

One of the best ways to move from a meaningless discussion to a meaningful one is to learn how to ask insightful questions. This doesn't mean your goal is to get the other person to share their most vulnerable, intimate secrets with you. However, you can take some steps to go beyond talking about their opinion of pizza toppings and their favorite movie. Eric's family used to love to play this old game from the '70s called "The Un-Game." You draw cards that contain insightful and interesting questions, and you choose which person in the group you want to ask. None of the questions are threatening—they don't probe into past hurts or deepest fears. But they are insightful, and they help the group get to know each other in a deeper way. Asking "Un-Game" types of questions, such as, "What's your favorite childhood memory?" or "What are you most looking forward to in this next year?" not only show a true interest in the other person's life, but open up great channels for deeper discussions.

Obviously, it can be awkward to ask these kinds of questions right after you say, "Hi, nice to meet you." But if you are sensitive to the other person as well as the leading of God's Spirit, you will find the right moments to help the conversation take a more meaningful turn.

Practice Elegant Speech

It's not necessary to sound like a British aristocrat or a flowery, old-fashioned poet to excel at the art of elegant speech. It's more than possible to be relaxed and feel like yourself in a conversation while still expressing yourself with dignity and grace. However, the lackluster, rude, and ungracious manner in which many of us communicate does not reflect the glory of our King. Colossians 4:6 says, "Let your speech be always with grace, seasoned with salt." And Christ says we will answer to God for every idle word that proceeds out of our mouth (Matthew 12:36). Scripture is full of warnings and exhortations regarding our words and our speech, so it's certainly an area worth evaluating before God. Here are a few questions to ask yourself:

- Do I use crude humor or make sexually inappropriate comments?
- Do I gossip, criticize, or belittle others with my words?

- Do I use profanity or substitutions for profanity that make me sound crass and disrespectful? (Example: Not long ago I encountered a group of Christian young women who used "substitute" cuss words in their prayers and conversations in place of more graphic terms. True, they weren't cussing, but the implication was more than clear to everyone who heard it. They weren't intentionally meaning to be crass, but the use of these few little words reduced the young women from being gracious and ladylike to sounding like crude, immature teenagers. It created a disrespectful and irreverent tone and certainly did not bring honor to the name of Christ.)

- Do I overuse filler words such as *like, really,* or *and stuff?* Filler words clutter up conversation and make you sound less intelligent than you are. And when giving any kind of public presentation, nothing makes you sound unprofessional like an overabundance of fillers.

- Do I mumble or talk too softly, as if I'm ashamed of what I have to say? Remember that we are to be ambassadors of Christ, and instead of sheepishly muttering, we are to boldly and confidently speak the truth in love.

- Do I ramble or talk too fast, especially when I feel nervous or awkward?

- Do I talk so loud that everyone in the room is forced to listen to me whether they want to or not?

If you answered yes to any of the above, ask God to equip you to remake your habits in these areas. Begin to observe women who excel at the art of gracious and elegant speech. Study what the Bible has to say about the words that come out of your mouth. And make a purposeful, prayerful effort to use your tongue only for the glory of God. You'll be amazed at the difference these things make in your ability to showcase social grace.

Show Respect to Those You Live With

As I mentioned earlier, many couples assume that the moment they take their wedding vows is the moment they are free to be slobs around each other. But throwing dignity to the wind in your closest relationships shows an incredible amount of selfishness and lack of respect to them. Your spouse, parents, siblings, and best friends are some of the most important people in your life. Why treat them as less valuable than a stranger at the local coffee shop?

Whether you are married or single, now is the perfect time to begin maintaining dignity in your closest relationships—especially the people you live with. While it is certainly not something to get uptight or stressed over, showing basic honor and respect to the people you live with can go a long way in keeping those relationships strong and healthy.

Eric and I have been married for 14 years, and we have always made it a high priority to treat each other with respect, even to this day. We sit up straight, make eye contact, and listen when the other person is talking to us, especially when something important is being expressed. We maintain good table manners, even when it is just the two of us eating together. We don't leave the bathroom door open when we are in there. We don't make bodily noises around each other. We put basic effort into our physical appearance, even when it's just the two of us at home all day. Rather than just rolling out of bed and sticking on a pair of grungy sweats, we take the time to make ourselves presentable for each other. We greet each other with an enthusiastic smile in the morning, and take time to ask how the other person is doing. It is our goal never to treat each other with the attitude, "Why should I be excited to see you? I'm around you every day."

These things may seem like basic, simple things to do, but they have gone a long way in keeping our marriage thriving and our romance alive and fresh.

I would encourage you to prayerfully examine the way you behave around the people closest to you. If there are any ways in which you could show them more honor and respect, ask God to equip you to do so. Just adding in a little dignity can go a long way in bringing freshness and appreciation back into a familiar relationship.

When it comes to excelling in manners, there is no cookie cutter pattern that will work in every situation. But if your intention in all situations is to reflect the glory of Christ and selflessly love and serve those around you, then you will soon discover how richly you can bless someone's life simply by being Christlike in the way you communicate.

5

BECOMING SOCIALLY SENSITIVE

Social Grace Secret #2

*Charm is deceitful and beauty is passing, but a
woman who fears the LORD, she shall be praised.*

PROVERBS 31:30

*I*t wasn't until I had a daughter that I began to fully realize how
much women are naturally wired to use their feminine wiles in
clever and strategic ways. My little girl, Harper, who is almost two, is
one of the most adorable children on the planet. (I can say this without sounding overly prideful because we adopted her from Korea!)
The problem is that she *knows* she's adorable. She constantly attempts
to use her feminine charm to get her own way. If she wants a cookie,
she'll plead, "Cookie?" and display the cutest, most heart-melting pout
on her chubby cheeks. If I am busy cleaning up the kitchen and she
wants to be held, she'll sidle up to my leg and croon in her most pitiful,

helpless-puppy voice, "Mama? Up, pweese!" If she wants to protest being left with a babysitter, she'll wrap her arms tightly around my neck and snuggle up against me with a forlorn expression, as if to say, "How can you possibly bear to leave such a sweet and cuddly child like me?" It's all very calculated and clever.

Though we enjoy Harper's cuteness, Eric and I have been very careful not to allow her charms to manipulate us. We never allow her to get her way when she uses these tactics. (Though I can't say the same for grandparents, family friends, and even strangers at the grocery store. People we don't even know frequently offer her candy or toys simply by seeing her tilt her head and grin at them.) But the amazing thing to me is that Harper somehow intrinsically knows how to use her femininity to twist someone's arm without ever being taught. Eric and I view these formative years as an opportunity to train Harper how to use her femininity to serve rather than manipulate. Her little pout might seem adorable at the age of two, but it certainly will *not* be adorable at the age of sixteen. No matter how cute or innocent it seems now, it's merely an evidence of her flesh at work, using her femininity for selfish purposes. That's why this attitude needs to be removed through loving training and discipline.

But for all too many of us, these attitudes weren't dealt with at a young age, and we grew into scheming, self-focused, manipulative young women. Proverbs 31:30 says, "Charm is *deceitful*" (emphasis added). When we use our feminine qualities—such as our affection, our physical appearance, our personality, and our emotions—for selfish purposes, we become deceitful and manipulative. Often without even realizing it, we try to control the people around us by the way we act. Instead of serving and meeting others' needs, we are constantly in a power play for attention, approval, and position. And as I've said, we cannot reflect the glory of Christ when we are vying for the glory of self.

Scripture makes very clear the fact that deceitful feminine charm does not lead to true beauty. In order to become socially sensitive to those around us, we must learn to submit our feminine attributes to the Spirit of God rather than to the control of our flesh. Before we look at some of the practical ways that we can excel at the art of social sensitivity, manipulation and selfishness must be purged from our existence. Let's take a closer look at three key ways to cultivate social sensitivity into our lifestyle.

Flee Manipulation

Over the years I've heard about, seen the effects of, and personally encountered many cases of manipulative femininity. But for the sake of our discussion, I'd like to highlight two examples in particular—two young women who demonstrated their schemes in completely opposite ways, but with the same root agenda...to glorify self.

The first young woman (we'll call her Brandi) initially seemed like a loving, outward-focused girl. She was bubbly, friendly, and full of laughter and fun. But after a few times of being around her, I began to notice that Brandi dominated every social situation. Her center stage personality, nonstop joking, and overly loud giggle demanded that everyone in the room pay attention to her. She was charming, to be sure, and even loads of fun to be around. She made people laugh. However, I couldn't help but realize that at every prayer gathering or dinner, the entire group would spend the majority of the time listening to Brandi carry on—and every conversation she was part of always centered around *her.* She continually built herself up—talking about her large circle of friends or the different guys who were interested in her. But she somehow did it subtly enough that it didn't seem like overt bragging. And she complimented others just enough to keep people from noticing her extreme focus on self. She displayed just enough "humility" to deflect the fact that she was arrogant and self-consumed.

The quieter people in the group were overlooked when Brandi was around. In the rare moments when someone else took the lead in conversation, Brandi never stuck around to listen. Instead, she would sidle up to someone in the group and begin whispering to them, often pulling them into another room where she could control and dominate the conversation. And in the few times when no one paid attention to her, she became a different person. She would sulk off with her cell phone, texting other friends and acting sullen and moody—making everyone around her feel that they had somehow offended her.

Every so often Brandi would acknowledge her overbearing manner by saying things like, "I wish I weren't so loud and so outgoing—but God made me this way! I just can't help it. People just need to deal with it. This is the way I am." It was obvious she did not feel the need to change.

Soon it became known that Brandi was not only being self-focused and disrespectful in public, but she was also using her manipulative schemes in private—spreading rumors, false accusations, and gossip among her circle of Christian friends at an alarming rate in order to gain (or maintain) a position of control over others. What started out simply as a bit of selfish insensitivity had morphed into a messy web of deceit and broken trust. It was a clear example of how manipulation can quickly grow from a little flame to an out-of-control fire, destroying lives and relationships in its wake.

The second young woman was very different than Brandi. We'll call her Stacey. Instead of being loud and in-your-face, she was reclusive and shy. She seemed to loathe personal attention. She never wanted to be asked a question in a social situation. She would hang in the background and keep to herself. She seemed troubled and depressed, and she eluded to a dark and abusive past. She never took center stage. She was quiet and respectful. She seemed to be really blessed when others took an interest in her life. She also seemed to be growing in her relationship with God and deepening her relationship with other Christian young women.

Stacey had some severe health and emotional problems, apparently tied to some abuse she had suffered in her past. She told her close Christian friends that she desperately desired to be set free from these things. Often her friends would minister to her throughout the night, staying by her side and crying out to God for her healing and deliverance.

A few times she collapsed on the street and ended up in the hospital, and they would all get out of bed in the middle of the night to be there by her side, loving her and ministering to her around the clock. She was always extremely grateful and very apologetic that her issues were taking so much of her friends' time and energy.

After a few months of pouring themselves out for Stacey and spending many nights wrestling in prayer for her, her friends began to notice a subtle shift in the intensity of her health problems. They didn't get better. In fact, they got worse and worse to the point where the devoted little group was ministering to her needs on a nearly full-time basis. They weren't able to focus on much else because Stacey's crisis was so urgent, intense, and physically demanding.

One weekend Stacey's health problems reached a peak. Her friends took turns staying with her for four days straight, day and night. But in spite of how much they prayed, things kept getting worse and worse. They were exhausted and discouraged. They began to seek advice from trusted Christian leaders. Some insight from a pastor brought a shocking revelation.

"I think she's lying," the pastor said after hearing about Stacey. "I don't thing she really has these problems. I think she's making the whole thing up just to get attention."

Her friends struggled to digest that possibility. "If I didn't know Stacy so well," one of them said, "I'd come to that conclusion too. But she has always seemed like the last person in the world who would try to get attention. She's always been so shy and reclusive."

"That could just be part of her manipulation over others," the pastor suggested. "Sometimes deceitful people are incredible actors."

He turned out to be right on. When they confronted her, they discovered that Stacey's extreme displays of health problems had merely been ploys for attention. Stacey had been an unbelievable actress. She had even fooled doctors and nurses at the hospital on numerous occasions.

Once again, it was selfish female manipulation at its worst. She took advantage of people's time, resources, and friendship. She had worked her way into a position of control—dominating others' love, energy, and focus. And the mess she left in her wake was devastating. Trust was shattered, faith was shaken, and friendships were broken.

Just as guys have a natural propensity toward lust, women often have a natural bent to manipulate and control others. Whether it takes the form of a center stage personality, clever playacting, or merely using subtlety and charm to twist someone's arm, manipulation is something we all need to be vigilantly on the lookout for. As I said, when a sweet-looking two-year-old uses a pretty pout to get her way, it seems harmless and funny. But when manipulation is given the opportunity to grow and develop in a girl's life, it becomes repulsive, ugly, and relentlessly destructive—not only to her life, but to the many other lives she affects.

It's impossible to reflect the glory of Jesus Christ while being controlling and manipulative. Allow the Spirit of God to gently reveal any ways in which you have been allowing manipulation into your life and behavior, in big or small ways. Here are a few questions that might help get you started:

- Do I use my physical appearance to get attention?
- Do I use my personality to draw people's focus to myself?
- Do I play emotional games to gain control over others (being moody, giving people the silent treatment when I'm upset, etc)?
- Do I use gossip or criticism to gain control over others?
- Do I continually turn the topic of conversation to focus on me?
- Do I notice the quiet people around me, or am I too busy taking center stage?
- Is the motive of my heart to bring glory to Jesus Christ or to gain attention and approval for myself?

You may find it helpful to write down anything God speaks to your heart. If you discover any level of manipulation in your life, big or small, ask God to forgive you, cleanse you, and purge it from your life by the power of His Spirit. Ask Him to retrain your habits and attitudes. You may even want to write down specific ideas for how you can begin behaving differently in certain relationships or situations. Consider recruiting the help of a trusted, godly accountability partner. Meet with this person regularly to pray about this area of your life and talk through the ways in which God is helping you change and grow. Remember, no matter how enslaved to wrong patterns you might feel, God is more than capable of transforming a controlling, manipulative female into a radiant, selfless, shining example of His beauty. All you must do is fully yield to His work.

Reach Out to the Lonely

Christ spoke (and lived) a very clear message about being socially selfless. He said,

> When you give a dinner or a supper, do not ask your friends, your brothers, your relatives, nor rich neighbors, lest they also invite you back, and you be repaid. But when you give a feast, invite the poor, the maimed, the lame, the blind. And you will be blessed, because they cannot repay you; for you shall be repaid at the resurrection of the just (Luke 14:12-14).

The pattern of God's kingdom is completely opposite from the pattern of this world. God's kingdom is not about self-promotion, hobnobbing, or gaining social status and attention. It's about a life poured out for the least, the lost, the outcast. If we desire to reflect the stunning beauty of Christ, we must live according to His pattern. Instead of seeing social get-togethers as a chance to win friends and gain favor, we are to use them as an opportunity to bless and serve those who are overlooked by society. One of the very best ways to be socially selfless is to let God's Spirit train you how to see the lonely ones around you and learn how to reach out to them.

It's easy and fun to hang around the confident, outgoing, life-of-the-party types of people. And just as Christ said, in spending time with the popular, well-respected people of the group, you are able to build up your own approval rating and gain more friends. However, it requires a lot of sacrifice and selflessness to spend the entire time off in a corner unnoticed, reaching out to an isolated social outcast who can't do anything for your popularity status. Lots of times these are the people no one really wants to spend time with. They are challenging to be around. They don't know how to engage in interesting conversation. They are lonely and insecure—and it shows. They aren't always fun to be with. But they desperately need to be shown the love of Christ.

I will never forget observing my brother-in-law, Mark, during his senior year of high school. We attended the largest, wealthiest, and snobbiest high school in the state. Popularity and status were everything. Mark had no trouble making friends. His winning blue eyes and super-friendly personality made him instantly rise to the top of the social ladder. He was well known and well liked, even in a school of more than 4000 students. But right before his senior year, Mark had an experience that forever changed his life. He went on an extended missionary venture, and God radically altered him. He became sold out for Jesus Christ. And his priorities completely changed. When he returned to high school for his senior year, he was no longer interested in popularity. He was only interested in being an extension of Christ's love to those in need.

Rather than spending time with all his popular friends, Mark chose to reach out to the outcasts—the foreign exchange students no one ever talked to, the special-needs students everyone else overlooked or made fun of, the shy and awkward kids who always hung back in the corners. Time and time again, I would see Mark unashamedly sitting with these people, showing a genuine interest in their lives and not caring what anyone else thought of him. At the end of that year, Mark had lost a lot of his former popularity ranking, but he had made an eternal impact upon the lives of many who would never have seen the love of Christ if not for his obedience.

When I was in third grade, I moved to a new school halfway through the year. I didn't know anyone, and the circles of friends had already formed. At that point in my life, I was friendly and outgoing, and I didn't have any trouble making new friends. So within a few weeks I was surrounded by an accepting group of new pals, but I noticed one red-haired girl named Heather who was always left out. No one seemed to like her or want to talk with her. I told my mom about her, and she encouraged me to reach out to her. "Use the influence God has given you," she told me. "If you are nice to her, maybe your other friends will begin treating her better as well." So I tried it. I smiled at her, talked to her, and invited her to join our games on the playground. Soon, all my other friends were following my example, and Heather was accepted and included.

I didn't think much about this experience until several years later, when I had moved out of state and received a letter from Heather. She said that my taking the time to reach out to her in third grade had changed her life. Up until then, no one had ever treated her with value, but after I had reached out to her, she finally felt loved for the first time in her life. It gave her confidence to make friends and thrive socially. And she believed that she was still reaping the benefits of what I had done, even years later. I was amazed. I'd had no idea one simple act of kindness could so radically transform someone's life.

That little lesson has stayed with me. On many occasions when I see a lonely or left-out person, I've remembered Heather and thought, *If I don't reach out to this person, who will?* A great principle to remember is that small acts of selflessness can change lives for eternity.

Take some time to prayerfully consider your behavior toward the "unlovable" or "outcasts" that you encounter. Do you notice them, or are you too caught up in promoting your own popularity to see the lonely lives around you? Are you willing to sacrifice your social status and personal comfort in order to reach out to those everyone else overlooks? If you feel resistant toward this idea, ask God to change your heart and make you willing. If you feel awkward and don't know where to start, ask Him to direct you. Often just noticing a lonely person, smiling, asking their name, and showing genuine interest in who they are will go a long, long way in bringing joy to that person's life.

Remember not to compare yourself to those around you. When everyone else is completely consumed with promoting their own image and popularity, it's easy to fall into the same trap without even realizing it. But God has called us to a different pattern. We must follow His example alone.

Become Selfless Toward Guys

When it comes to interacting with guys, we women have two choices—to be selfish or selfless. Unfortunately, most young women are extremely selfish toward guys. Our culture trains us to use our feminine charm to manipulate, control, and seduce men. Many of us only know how to be flirtatious, seductive, and calculating toward guys because we've never seen it done any other way. But it's more than possible to treat guys with respect and selflessness—not using our femininity to defraud, but to honor and inspire. It just requires a shift in attitude. It means seeing guys as brothers to encourage and motivate rather than as potential boyfriends or opportunities to get male attention. It means being friendly without being a flirt, being encouraging without being manipulative, and being a reflection of Christ's beauty instead of a reflection of this culture's twisted priorities.

Being selfless toward guys also means letting them be *guys*. Our society encourages women to be forward, aggressive, and in-your-face toward men. But God has designed men to initiate and women to respond. In the long run, we'll be far happier if we follow His pattern instead of this world's. As I discussed in *Answering the Guy Questions,* I have yet to meet a woman who wants to marry a wimpy, insecure man who refuses to take the lead in the relationship. And yet all too often young women strip a man of his masculinity before the romance even begins. Instead of patiently allowing him to woo and win her heart, she takes the lead and robs him of his God-given position. He may appear to like it at first—after all, it saves him from going to all the work of pursuing her. But in the end he'll lose respect for both her and for himself, and the relationship will be set according to a faulty pattern.

It is not easy to be selfless in our interactions toward guys, especially while living in a culture that continually pushes an opposite message upon us. But if you ask God to equip you to reflect His beauty in this area of your life, He will guide and direct your steps. I've met many beautiful, radiant, Christlike, set-apart young women who are amazing examples when it comes to interacting with guys. They aren't shy and insecure around the opposite sex; rather, they are friendly and encouraging toward the guys in their life. But they are never forceful, critical, or flirtatious. Their goal is to draw guys' attention and focus toward Christ and not themselves. And the result is a refreshing display of male/female interaction as God intended it to be. God's Word exhorts young men to treat the "younger women as sisters, with all purity" (1 Timothy 5:2). The way we act around guys either assists or hinders them in following this pattern.

Prayerfully ask God to reveal any ways in which you have been behaving selfishly toward guys. And then, by the power of His Spirit, let him reshape and remake your habits in this area. Soon you'll be on the path to building the Christlike warrior-poets of the future. (To go far more in-depth into this subject, I'd suggest my book *Answering the Guy Questions.*)

6

DRESSING WITH SELFLESS STYLE

Social Grace Secret #3

Modesty is the ancient secret of allure.

CHRISTA TAYLOR

The way we dress sends a message to those around us, whether we mean to or not. A girl who flaunts her body with short, tight outfits sends the message that she wants guys to notice her. A girl who dresses like a slob sends the message that she does not care enough about those around her to give any thought to her appearance. A girl who hides behind shapeless, dowdy clothes sends the message that she is ashamed of her femininity. And a girl who dresses with modest, feminine, dignified style sends the message that she values those around her and wants to reflect the beauty of Christ in her appearance.

Christa Taylor, a young Christian clothing designer, expressed it this way:

When a young woman chooses to dress in a way that thought-lessly exposes her body or, worse, seeks to use her body to allure men sexually, she is reducing herself to mere eye candy. All that is truly good and beautiful and unique about a young woman is lost, and she is only seen as an object for sex. Wom-anhood today is so crude, largely because of the attack on female modesty. Many mainstream fashion trends are very unflattering. Low-rise jeans, for instance, can create "muffin tops" and, when seated, reveal way too much of your derri-ere to the unfortunate individual behind you. This does not enhance a women's beauty or attractiveness. In contrast, a woman who is dressed with dignity and grace, in feminine apparel that flatters, draws attention to her face, her person-ality, and charm.

Modesty is the ancient secret of allure. An oxymoron? I think not. When women choose to dress with modesty and dignity, it just might flip everything around...We were created in such a way that when we humans act without restraint and without any rules, we don't have as much fun! Modesty and dignity helps women protect their romantic hopes, challenges men to be courteous and honorable, and will turn the whole sexual revolution on its head. That is something to look forward to.[1]

I mentioned earlier that when Eric first attempted to put words to the idea of set-apart femininity, he described it as a blend between Audrey Hepburn dignity (not mere physical charm) and Amy Car-michael selflessness. When you combine loveliness and dignity with selflessness and sacrifice, you see a vision of feminine beauty as God intended it to be. That's the attitude that should be reflected in our appearance.

As I said earlier, women in certain Christian circles have adopted the idea that it is God-honoring to cover up their feminine beauty, as if being drab and dowdy is somehow more spiritual. While I certainly agree that flaunting our bodies is not honoring to God, I do not at all agree that true modesty hides a woman's feminine beauty. On the contrary, as Christa Taylor explained, true modesty actually *enhances* a woman's feminine beauty, grace, and ladylike qualities. But rather than drawing attention to the sensual areas of her body, true modesty draws attention to a young woman's face, eyes, radiance, and smile— and saves the sensual part of her beauty as a gift for her spouse in marriage.

In previous books I've talked about the principle of feminine mystique. *Mystique* means keeping sacred things sacred. When a woman carelessly exposes her body, her heart, and her most intimate secrets to anyone and everyone she meets, she strips herself of all mystery, intrigue, and fascination. Nearly all of the godly young men I've talked to have expressed that a young woman who is guarded and mysterious captivates them far more than one who is aggressive, seductive, and easy to get.

There is a big difference between dressing modestly and dressing with feminine mystique. It's possible to dress modestly and yet not exude any feminine mystique at all; think of women you have seen who wear shapeless, drab, frumpy clothing and keep a dour expression on their makeup-less faces as a statement of being pious. That's not dressing with selflessness. Rather, it sends the message "I am more spiritual because I am covering up every bit of feminine beauty I possess. I am wearing this grim and gloomy expression on my face because I want you to notice how pious I am." They may not be flaunting their figures, but they are still attempting to draw attention to themselves. On the other hand, some women cover up their feminine beauty out of insecurity rather than the desire to be seen as godly—if that's you, then it's important to learn who you are in Christ and allow Him to heal your heart of past hurts and wounds. *Authentic Beauty* speaks to this issue.

But a woman who exudes true feminine mystique is both modest and selfless. She doesn't hide her femininity; she dresses to reflect the joy and radiance that fill her soul. She dresses to honor her husband, or future husband, and the men around her. Her outward beauty is an expression of the transformation Christ has made to her inner life. She puts effort into her appearance, not to gain approval and attention, but to show respect and honor to those she interacts with. Her goal is to point people's eyes to Jesus and not to herself. She is modest and beautiful at the same time. In fact, her modesty is part of what makes her so beautiful and fascinating.

Let's explore some practical principles of dressing with selfless style.

Showcase Heaven's Beauty

When Catherine Booth, cofounder of the Salvation Army, began to prayerfully consider her outward appearance, she said this:

> It seemed clear to me from the teaching of the Bible that Christ's people should be separate from the world in everything which denoted character and that they should not only be separate but appear so. As I advanced in religious experience I became more and more convinced that my appearance ought to be such as to show everybody with whom I came in contact that I have renounced the pomp and vanities of the world, and that I belonged to Christ.[2]

Amy Carmichael wrote about several young Indian women who became followers of Christ and decided to give up their jewels—a decision that was completely outrageous to Indian culture at that time. A woman's jewels were her security, her identity, her way of being accepted by society. And yet God was challenging these young Indian Christians to become dead to the world and its applause. Amy described the choice of one young woman:

> It was a tremendous decision she made at the foot of the Cross that day. But nothing anyone could say could shake her. She had seen her Beloved, her Redeemer. On His brow

was a crown not of gold, but of thorns. His hands and His feel were not jeweled, but pierced. She had seen Him. Could she follow Him adorned with gold?[3]

Rather than showcasing the status and sparkle of the world, these women desired to shine with the radiance of Christ.

This is the foundational principle of dressing selflessly—to dress as a daughter of the King rather than a product of pop culture. To lay down our pursuit of gaining the approval and applause of this world, and to live for His smile alone.

Take some time to prayerfully consider the way you dress and what your inner motives are. Does your appearance show everyone that you belong to Christ, as Catherine Booth said, or does it show everyone that you belong to this world? Are there any "jewels" Christ might be asking you to lay aside in order to better reflect His glory? Your "jewels" might be your addiction to the latest trends, your controlling craving for designer jeans and sunglasses, or even your obsession with always having the latest technology (cell phone, laptop, etc.) in order to show it off everywhere you go. There might not be anything intrinsically wrong with a pair of designer jeans or a brand new iPhone—but too many of us have made these things part of our status and identity. Are we willing to let them go, that our identity might be found in Christ alone?

Here are a few key questions to ask yourself:

- Does the way I dress place value on the status symbols and materialism of this world?

- Am I so consumed with keeping my look up-to-date that I spend an inordinate amount of time and energy shopping for the latest trends? Am I insecure and uncomfortable if I'm not wearing the latest fads?

- Do I secretly look down on people who are not wearing the most current styles?

- Is there anything in my appearance that is sending the wrong message to the world about what my true priorities are?

Remember, it is more than possible to dress stylishly without being enslaved to worldly trends and status symbols. (As I said, there is nothing more spiritual about being frumpy!) However, it's important to recognize that it is not a woman's clothing or sense of style that truly gives her grace and dignity—but the Christlike radiance that exudes from her inner being. In light of eternity, things like clothes and jewelry are trivial and meaningless. They are tools that can be used to serve a higher purpose in our life—our call to reflect Jesus Christ to this world. But the moment we become servants of clothes, trends, style, or possessions is the moment we stop serving Christ and start serving ourselves instead.

Many set-apart female missionaries throughout history chose to lay down personal style and adopt the simple clothing styles of the people they were ministering to in order to keep their appearance from being a distraction to the Gospel.

Lottie Moon, a young single missionary to China in the early 1900s, was described as a pretty woman with lovely soft features, kind eyes, and dark hair that she wore high swept. Raised in a wealthy Southern family, she was used to American luxuries and style. But on the mission field, she willingly chose to live like those she wished to reach for Christ:

> She began to look Chinese as she went into the villages, for she dressed in a plain Chinese coat and gown and wore embroidered shoes made from fragments of old garments. Later she estimated that her shoes cost less than eighty cents and her winter boots less than a dollar. She slept on a brick bed and ate food bought in a village market, and cooked in Chinese kettles.[4]

When Amy Carmichael was a young missionary to Japan (before she arrived in India) she had an experience that profoundly influenced her. She was sharing the Gospel with an old woman, and just when the woman seemed ready to turn to Christ in faith, she noticed Amy's hands. It was very cold that day, and Amy was wearing fur gloves. The opportunity to win a soul for Christ was lost because of it. Amy wrote,

> I went home, took off my English clothes, put on my Japanese kimono and never again, I trust, risked so much for the sake of so very little.[5]

When it comes to the way we dress, are we placing value on the temporary things of the world rather than the eternal treasures of God's kingdom? Are we bypassing opportunities to be ambassadors for Christ because we are too busy flaunting worldly style and status?

Before we can truly learn how to dress with selfless style, we must first become dead to the world and its applause. Once we exchange the world's value system for Christ's eternal priorities, we can begin to reflect the beauty of heaven.

Dress with Dignity

In today's world most modern girls either dress seductively or like slobs. But once upon a time, women wore elegant, feminine clothes and carried themselves with dignity and poise. The true gentlemen of yesteryear were not enticed by sensual outfits; rather, they were captivated by true beauty and feminine grace. When a lady walked into the room, he noticed the sparkle of her eye and the radiance of her smile, not the outline of her body. But "dressing like a lady" is a lost concept these days. The Proverbs 31 woman (whom I wrote about in great detail in my book *Set-Apart Femininity*) is the epitome of feminine beauty and feminine valiance. She is clothed in "strength and dignity" (Proverbs 31:25 NASB). She makes coverings for herself of "fine linen and purple" (verse 22). She has the respect of her children and community, and she has captured the heart of her husband. When a young woman dresses with the grace and dignity of a true lady, she gains the *right* kind of attention from the *right* kind of guys.

Dressing with dignity doesn't mean giving up being feminine or attractive. Rather, it means exchanging the culture's cheap counterfeit of feminine appeal for the stunning, *God*-designed version of female allure. And by the way, Christ-built men aren't just looking for girls who purposely drab-down their feminine beauty or hide behind tent-like clothes. They desire to see young women who exude a loveliness and graceful feminine beauty that flows from the inside out; a feminine dignity that is both modest and stunningly, refreshingly beautiful.

The typical style of dress for today's young women is anything but elegant or refined. While I'm certainly not a proponent of stuffy, fussy outfits, I also believe that most modern young women are in need of a bit more class. Typically, the only reason we dress in anything nicer than jeans and a T-shirt is when we absolutely have to. Our American obsession with being super-casual has led to an overall sloppiness in our daily appearance—and when we adopt this pattern we exude a message of carelessness rather than one of dignity and grace.

There is a big difference in how I feel on days when I've dressed hurriedly in sweats than on days when I put effort into my appearance. When I am dressed sloppily, I am more prone to *feel* sloppy, lethargic, and unmotivated as I go about my daily tasks. But dressing with dignity brings value to the things I'm working on. It reminds me, "This work is important. It is deserving of my best attention and focus."

The way I'm dressed also affects the way I sit, stand, and carry myself. If I'm just in a slipshod outfit, I tend to slouch more and carry myself with far less poise than if I'm dressed a bit nicer. Dressing with class reminds me to carry myself with dignity and grace at all times. It keeps me focused on maintaining good manners and etiquette. It also shows honor to those I live with, as mentioned earlier. If I dress haphazardly around my husband and kids, and only make myself look nice when we go out to meet other people, I'm sending the message that my family is not as worthy of my efforts as other people are;

that I don't feel like going to the trouble of making myself look good for those closest to me.

I'm always disturbed when I observe homemakers who habitually look like slobs, using the justification, "Why should I bother looking nice? I'm just hanging out with kids all day long." This attitude disregards the *value* of guiding a home and caring for a family. I've observed that when a mother dresses with dignity, she takes her role far more seriously, and the work she is doing begins to actually feel valuable and important.

Of course, there are always exceptions to this principle. As mentioned earlier, clothing should be a *tool* to serve God's purposes in our lives. There will be times when God's priorities or life circumstances demand that we forgo taking time on our appearance and turn our attention to more important things. It is not something to ever become worried or stressed about. Remember, it's not ultimately the clothes we wear, but the inner beauty of Christ that creates our dignity and loveliness. Even in a filthy concentration camp, a truly set-apart woman radiates with beauty that does not fade no matter how dingy her appearance becomes—because her beauty flows from the life of Christ within her.

But whenever we *do* have a choice, let's honor our King and those around us by exchanging the sloppy, careless, trashy style of the culture for a classier approach to our appearance. Just to help make this even more practical, let me share some specific ways I personally apply this principle. (And please remember these are simply my own personal guidelines and not a foolproof prescription for everyone.)

Typically, I choose to wear stylish feminine outfits instead of casual jeans and T-shirts, even if I'm just working at home or I'm with my family. This doesn't mean I'm in a dress and high heels everyday! With four little children to manage, my clothes have to be functional and comfortable. I've found that just a few feminine upgrades to my outfits can make a huge difference in taking me from sloppy to classy. For instance, wearing tailored, trouser-style jeans and pants that are a bit dressier than the form-fitting low-cut style. (Tailored jeans are also more modest.) You can usually find young, stylish pants and jeans of this kind in the "young professional" stores at the mall—stores that cater to young, working twentysomethings rather than just teens. Also, I've found dark-wash jeans usually look more polished than lighter shades.

Wearing a short casual jacket and button-up top or a dressier feminine blouse with jeans is a great way to add a bit of class without feeling super dressed up. And in the summer, wearing a casual flowy skirt with a simple feminine top is a great way to keep cool and feel refined at the same time. In fact, I've started adding more casual skirts to my wardrobe because I've discovered it's a great way to maintain my feminine dignity and still feel casual and comfortable.

As I said, there are always exceptions. I do have days when it's just easier and more practical to wear sweats or casual jeans and a T-shirt—like when I'm cleaning out the basement or baking cookies with the kids. But for the most part, I feel and act more dignified when I dress like a lady. So I make it my goal to do so whenever possible.

I am not the kind of woman who wears piles of makeup, heavy perfume, false eyelashes, or long, curvy fingernails. Nearly all of my jewelry, including my wedding ring, is simple and understated. I don't like to be over-done. I feel that women who try to be overly glamorous usually come across as tacky, not classy. But on the other hand, I feel that the plain-Jane, drab hair, no-makeup, earthy-granola style comes across a bit dour and dreary. I want my appearance to reflect the joy, color, radiance, and *life* that Christ has given me. And that's what I keep in mind when it comes to basic grooming.

My goal is that makeup would enhance—not overpower—my eyes and smile. I typically wear simple jewelry (usually with sentimental value) that accents, rather than overwhelms, my femininity. I keep my hair cut in a style that frames my face—and I try to wash and style it every day instead of carelessly throw it back in a clip. (With four little ones, this doesn't always happen!) I try to choose clothes that are rich with color rather than lifeless and dull. I don't obsess over any of these things, but here is my basic code of conduct when it comes to grooming and accessorizing: *to enhance my natural feminine beauty and reflect the simple joy of Christ.*

Honor Guys by Dressing Modestly

Dressing with selfless dignity means not giving other guys the pleasure of viewing what was only meant for your husband. It means honoring and respecting your future spouse by keeping your body sacred and set-apart for his eyes only. And it means respecting the men around you by not putting temptation right in front of their noses, and then blaming them for viewing you like a sex object. Again, it doesn't mean hiding behind a long, tentlike robe. It just means being guarded with how much of your body is being exposed.

Here is the rule of thumb that works for me on where to draw the line when it comes to showing skin: Any area of my body that can be associated with sensuality is not to be touched *or* seen by anyone other than my husband. For example, if someone touches me on the elbow, there isn't anything sensual about it. In fact, often at weddings or fancy restaurants, an usher or waiter will take me by the arm and lead me to my seat. Eric has no reason to be concerned about this kind of interaction because there's nothing sexual about it. But if a guy came up and touched me on the thigh or put his hand on my stomach, it's a completely different story. Eric would have every reason to be jealous, angry, and hurt because that kind of touch can definitely be associated with sensuality.

Any area of my body that would be awkward or uncomfortable for another guy to touch is an area of my body I keep hidden for my husband's eyes alone. Upper chest, thighs, stomach—these might seem like harmless areas to show off, but if you were married and wanted to stay that way, you wouldn't allow another guy to touch you in any of those places. So why would you allow another guy to have the privilege of looking at what was meant for your husband's pleasure alone?

When you keep your husband's feelings at the forefront of your mind when deciding what to wear, the issue of how much skin to show becomes far less complicated.

Lots of young women I know frequently wear clothes that conceal almost every bit of skin on their body, and yet their outfits are anything but modest. Tight and form-fitting clothes can be just as sensual (if not more so) as clothes that reveal a lot of skin. It's really the same rule of thumb that applies in this situation. Any area of your body that can be associated with sensuality shouldn't be viewed by other men—whether in showing skin or in superfitted form. A turtleneck might not show any skin whatsoever, but if it is extremely tight in the chest area, then you are leaving very little to the imagination for any guy who happens to look your way. The same goes with pants and skirts. They might cover every square inch of skin, but if they cling too snugly to your figure, you are giving guys the pleasure of viewing what was meant for only your husband's enjoyment.

As I said earlier, there are many stylish and looser-fitting pants that are feminine and flattering without giving away the farm. They may be hard to find in the teenybopper stores at the mall where every pair of jeans is labeled "ultra-low-cut-stretch," but the young professional styles often have some pretty good options. You may have to pay a bit more for them, but it's better to have one or two pairs of classy, feminine jeans or pants than a whole closet full of supertight ones that only get tighter every time you wash them. Make it your goal that when a guy looks at you, he will notice the light of Christ in your eyes and the radiance of your smile rather than being distracted by the outline of your body.

Along the same lines, be aware of the way you carry yourself. A young woman of mystery does not sprawl on the floor with her legs carelessly splayed, drape herself haphazardly over a countertop so that her blouse hangs open, or unconsciously pull at her panty line. Carrying yourself with poise sends the message that your femininity is valuable. It also commands respect from the guys you encounter. A woman who carries herself like a lady is far more apt to be *treated* like a lady. On the flip side, a woman who carries herself with carelessness is more apt to be treated with disrespect. Here are a few practical tips:

- When sitting in a skirt, cross your legs at the ankle or place your legs parallel and drop them to one side. (And when sitting down or standing up in a skirt, keep your legs together to avoid flashing your underwear!)

- When sitting in pants, place your feet together on the floor and keep your knees together, or cross your legs at the ankle.

- Practice good posture by always keeping your back straight and crossing your legs at the ankle. You will always look more like a lady in this position than if you are slouched or hunched.

- If you need to lean down, bend your knees and lower your body without bending at the waist, which might cause your shirt to hang open. Or, if you absolutely have to bend down, discreetly place your hand over your upper chest so that your shirt stays put.

Regain a Lost Art

Social grace is not merely a bonus or optional quality for a set-apart young woman. It's an outflow of a thriving spiritual life. Jesus said,

> You shall love the LORD your God with all your heart, with all your soul, and with all your mind. This is the first and great commandment. And the second is like it. You shall love your neighbor as yourself (Matthew 22:37-39).

When these two principles govern our inner life, then being socially selfless is a natural by-product. When our chief aim is to bring glory to Christ; when we are far more consumed with Him than the trivial things of this world; and when we learn to put others above ourselves— we will excel at the lost art of social grace.

On a recent missions trip to Haiti, my friend Annie was approached by an older woman who had observed her selflessly loving orphans and serving those in need. "You are so radiant!" the woman exclaimed. What a high compliment. To be seen for our Christlike radiance and selflessness—rather than contrived physical beauty or social status— is truly an honor that every set-apart young woman should desire to achieve.

7

SACRED BEAUTY

The Enchanting Mystery of a Guarded Woman

*Do not let your adornment be merely outward…
rather let it be the hidden person of the heart.*

1 Peter 3:3-4

Ask men what makes a woman beautiful, and the resounding answer is often *mystery*. Eric and I have talked with countless young men over the years, and when we get on the subject of what kind of girl is most attractive to them, these are the answers we commonly hear:

> "A woman who guards her heart."
> "A woman who isn't too easy to get."
> "A woman who doesn't throw herself at me."
> "A woman who makes me prove I'm worthy of her heart."

"A woman who exudes a quiet dignity in the way she acts and dresses."

Such responses seem counterintuitive in a culture that praises women who are sexually aggressive, loose, and uninhibited. And yet, if you think about the essence of love, sex, and romance, these answers make sense. Where is the fun in winning someone's heart if they've already thrown their most intimate secrets out on the table? How can a man be intrigued and captivated by a woman who has no mystery at all?

In her book *A Return to Modesty,* Wendy Shalit makes a compelling argument that preserving the erotic depends upon a sense of mystery and guardedness. She says that modesty protects and inspires the kind of allure that actually lasts. When a woman gives away everything and throws all guardedness to the wind, she quickly loses her appeal. There's nothing left to discover about her. Wendy writes about a man who became incredibly disillusioned with his girlfriend once she went topless on the beach while they were together. After a few minutes of being in shock over her audacity, he suddenly found that he was somewhat turned off. His girlfriend was no longer fascinating to him. "By taking off her top," he explained, "she had broken the spell."[1]

I think that must be what makes Jane Austen's love stories so heart-meltingly romantic. What makes those old-fashioned romances so compelling is their sense of mystery; tales of young women who were guarded and protective of their hearts (and bodies) being heroically wooed and won by gallant gentlemen who highly valued femininity.

When mystery is guarded, romance flourishes and lasts. When mystery is lost, romance quickly withers and dies. If a woman guards the sacred core of her femininity and allows a man to rise to the challenge of pursuing her, wooing her, and winning her heart over time, instead of thrusting it upon him too readily, his masculine strength will be tested and proven. If he has had to work hard to win her, he is far less likely to take her for granted. Rather, he will become the heroic protector he was created to be—laying down his life to preserve and nurture the heart of the princess he worked so hard to win. Even after marriage, mystery can, and should, be carefully guarded and preserved. Eric and I work hard to preserve the mystery in our relationship. Whenever possible, we dress nicely for each other, showcase respect and manners around each other, and maintain privacy in the bathroom. When sacred things are kept sacred, the flame of passion and romance remains alive and thriving.

Mystery cannot be separated from true feminine beauty. It's part of God's pattern for femininity. Proverbs 31 portrays a beautiful, dignified, intelligent, and mysterious woman who "is clothed with strength and dignity" (Proverbs 31:25 NIV) and who is "like the merchant ships, bringing her food from afar" (verse 14 NIV). Think about the significance of that statement. This woman's life is intriguing and mysterious, like great ships that come from an exotic, faraway land.

The New Testament paints a clear and inspiring vision of this very same kind of captivating femininity:

> Do not let your adornment be merely outward—arranging the hair, wearing gold, or putting on fine apparel—rather let it be the hidden person of the heart with the incorruptible beauty of a gentle and quiet spirit, which is very precious in the sight of God (1 Peter 3:3-4).

"A gentle and quiet spirit" refers to a woman who is gracious, peaceful, serene, and quietly dignified—a woman who does not scrape and claw to be noticed and appreciated, but one who is fully content and secure in her relationship with her King. A woman with a gentle demeanor and quiet confidence in Christ will naturally guard the "hidden person" of her heart because she understands what it means to protect the sacred. A woman who lives according to God's pattern is captivating—because she stands out from among the throngs of women who are driven by selfishness and insecurity. As Song of Songs 2:2 says, "Like a lily among thorns, so is my darling among the maidens" (NIV). And as Proverbs 31:29 says, "Many women have done excellently, but you surpass them all" (RSV). A woman who possesses the incorruptible beauty of true feminine mystery will outshine all the rest.

When the Bible speaks of the "hidden person of the heart," it's talking about the secret, intimate part of who we are—the sacred core of our femininity. But if we embrace the "hold nothing back" version of womanhood we see all around us, we have no "hidden person of the heart" left to protect; everything we think, hope, dream, fear, and feel is all out there on display for the world to see. It's impossible to possess "the incorruptible beauty of a gentle and quiet spirit" if we follow the worldly pattern of femininity.

So just how do we as women protect the sacred core of our femininity in the midst of a culture that continually pressures us to throw all our mystery to the wind? I've talked with hundreds of young women who are confused about what it means to guard "the hidden person of the heart."

"Is it bad to have guys as friends?" they often ask. "How much should I share with a guy, and how much should I hold back and keep sacred? How do I protect feminine mystery and not come off as a snob?"

The reason that the concept of feminine mystery is hard to grasp is because in our modern era we've lost all understanding of protecting the sacred. Our global disregard for the sacred hasn't merely affected issues surrounding femininity. In nearly every sphere of life we have become haphazard and cavalier toward all that was once treated with reverence and respect.

For instance, just think about the way church has changed over the past few decades. People used to dress in their Sunday best to enter the house of God. Dressing up was a way of placing value, esteem, and honor upon their time of worship and gathering together with other believers. Now, most churches have become so informal that the majority of attendees are in their Saturday-morning hang-around-the-house clothes rather than their Sunday-morning best. The congregation wears jeans, and the pastor delivers his message in a laid-back Hawaiian shirt. Church worship used to be a distinguished art form; but now it is typically a noisy display of pop culture informality, performed by a handful of guitar-wielding twenty-year-olds with hip scruffy hair and grungy clothes. Sanctuaries used to be beautifully adorned with stained glass and mahogany pews. Now, they look like high school gymnasiums, with folding chairs and cheap, all-purpose flooring.

Don't get me wrong. I am not saying that dressing up or having a formal setting for church are the keys to true worship. It is certainly possible to experience the presence of God in a casual setting. I personally have had many great worship times in these kinds of environments. Formality is certainly not necessary for experiencing the presence of God. Many underground churches around the world are forced to hold meetings in cramped basements and abandoned buildings—and they experience the presence of God in powerful ways, far beyond what most of us have ever encountered. However, I believe that in America, our tendency toward the super-casual can sometimes lead to a lack of true reverence for the things of God; a lack of respect for the sacred. When our churches begin to portray Jesus as a casual buddy with a ponytail instead of the majestic King of all kings and Lord of all Lords that He is, we quickly lose the honor, respect, nobility, awe, and fear of God that is foundational to the Christian life.

Marriage is another sphere of life that has been greatly impacted by our lack of reverence for the sacred. God says that marriage "is to be held in *honor* among all" (Hebrews 13:4 NASB, emphasis added). He designed the joining together of two lives to be a sacred, holy covenant—unbreakable by anything but death. Malachi 2:13-14 describes God's anger toward those who do not take this holy covenant seriously:

> You cover the LORD's altar with tears, with weeping and groaning because He no longer regards the offering or accepts it with favor at your hand...because the LORD was witness to the covenant between you and the wife of your youth, to whom you have been faithless, though she is your companion and your wife by covenant (Malachi 2:13-14 RSV).

To God, divorce is an abomination. And yet the divorce rate among Christians has been actually *higher* than among non-Christians in many recent studies. We don't take our marriage covenants seriously anymore. We don't realize we are entering into a holy union before God. We behave selfishly and carelessly toward our spouse, and as soon as someone more appealing comes along, we are quick to forsake the one we pledged to love and serve for a lifetime. Even couples that stay together typically do not treat their marriage with reverence and respect. They take each other for granted. They allow sloppy, haphazard, disrespectful habits to creep into their relationship. They treat each other with dishonor. They complain about each other, embarrass each other, and make each other the brunt of jokes at social gatherings.

As I explained in *Answering the Guy Questions,* protecting the sacred was one of the key aspects to my God-written love story with Eric. When our romance was first blossoming, Eric spent several months away at missionary school. This was before the days of cell phones and email, if you can believe it. We could only talk on the phone about once a week and write each other letters. It may sound restrictive and old-fashioned, but to me it was a dream come true. Just think about what makes a Jane Austen romance so appealing. It's the slow, delicate process of one heart opening to another. In old-fashioned love stories you don't carelessly fling your mind, emotions, and body upon someone the moment they say they like you.

In fairy tales, you don't go from zero to sixty in seconds. Rather, you savor each conversation, carefully weigh each word, and patiently wait months or years before you finally win the priceless treasure of the other person's heart. Modern romances are sadly lacking in the dignity, nobility, and honor that was prevalent in the days of knights and fair maidens. The only way to gain the dignity and nobility that our feminine hearts crave is to carefully protect the sacred things, no matter how strange or old-fashioned they might seem.

Instead of spending mindless hours on the phone chitchatting with Eric every night, I waited with eager anticipation for his once-a-week call from the payphone outside his missionary school. Every word was savored. We didn't waste time talking about meaningless things. We cherished every moment and counted every conversation as significant because we only talked once a week. Instead of exchanging quick, shallow text messages every day, we took the time to write long, thoughtful letters to each other. I still love to look through the box of letters we wrote to each other during those years. I look at the carefully scripted, thoughtful words and remember the delicate way our hearts opened to each other. It was a thousand times more romantic and dignified than mindless emails or text messages.

This is not to say that you can't have the "Jane Austen magic" if you choose to use email or cell phones in your love story. The principle that makes the fairy-tale spirit come alive is keeping sacred things sacred.

Even now, after 14 years together, Eric and I make it our goal to keep our relationship sacred and treat our marriage with reverence. As I mentioned earlier, we treat each other with dignity and respect. We still write thoughtful, purposeful letters to each other—in fact, we even have special formal letterhead and scented stationary that we use specifically for this purpose. It might seem cheesy to some, but to us it is a simple way of keeping nobility in our love story.

Protecting the sacred is part of God's pattern. When sacred things are protected, marriages thrive, churches thrive, and culture thrives. The same is true for femininity. When sacred things are protected, feminine beauty and dignity are the natural by-product.

Being a Guardian of Your Heart

There is a big difference between a young woman who is careful and guarded in her femininity because she is afraid of doing something wrong, and a young woman who guards her femininity out of love for Jesus Christ and honor for her future husband. It's similar to the distinction between the woman who hides behind dull, drab, shapeless clothing in order to prove how "godly and modest" she is, and the woman who dresses with selfless, dignified elegance because she wants to bring glory to Jesus Christ. One is born out of humanly contrived self-effort. The other is born out of a passionate relationship with our Lord.

Hiding in a corner and refusing to look men in the eye or ever have a conversation with them is not truly protecting the sacred. Acting aloof and arrogant toward the opposite sex in the name of trying to "guard our heart" is not true feminine mystique. But neither is being haphazard and flippant with our heart and emotions, casually sharing our most vulnerable thoughts and intimate secrets with any Joe Blow who invites us out to coffee. A woman of honor is confident, friendly, and outward focused, and she does not draw attention to herself by either extreme shyness or extreme forwardness. She is willing and able to talk to guys, encourage guys, and build them up as brothers in Christ. She is confident and poised, she looks them in the eye, and she excels in the art of Christ-honoring conversation with them. And yet she does not quickly open up her heart to them. She is able to be a close sister and encourager without throwing the sacred core of her femininity to the wind.

My friend Annie, whom I mentioned earlier, is a great example of feminine mystique. She has a radiant smile and ready friendliness to all she comes in contact with, including guys. She is friendly and confident when she converses with the opposite sex, and yet if she ever senses that she is becoming the object of unhealthy male attention, she is quick to discreetly back away. When guy friends have pressured her to share more of her intimate thoughts than she is comfortable with, she has told them nicely but firmly that she doesn't feel comfortable opening up on that level. She isn't rude or stiff in response to inappropriate male behavior—she's just forthright and honest with them about her standards. Annie is a confident, radiant, beautiful, and guarded woman—and part of what makes her so lovely is her careful protection over what is most sacred in her life.

The Sacred Code of Honor

Eric recently spoke to a group of men about the code of honor and nobility by which every Christ-built man must live. In our modern era of male crudeness and lewdness, such a code seems oddly out of place—more appropriate for King Arthur and the Round Table than current American life. And yet Eric strongly believes this code of honor is one of the great keys to heavenly masculinity—and is a prime missing ingredient to true men of God being raised up in our day.

When a man exhibits true honor and nobility, specific qualities will mark his life. They comprise a sacred code of honor. A man who lives by this code will be:

- Dead to self-interest, confident in battle
- Courageous under fire
- Trained for war
- Restrained to the nature of God
- An upholder of decorum
- Harnessed of soul
- Unwilling to violate conscience
- A protector of the weak
- Marked by purity and virtue
- Unafraid of death
- Unwilling to be subjugated or debased
- The last to sleep and the first to rise
- Untouched by men's opinion
- A possessor of great inner stability
- Rightly prioritized

To live by God's sacred code of honor is the epitome of protecting the sacred. It's regaining the lost art of nobility and royal bearing. It's guarding the things God guards, and protecting the things He values. Just imagine what would happen to our society if men truly lived by this heavenly creed!

When Eric presented the code of honor to that group of Christian men, they were not only stirred and inspired, but also a bit daunted. Such regality sounded so extreme, so overly noble for our modern age. Was it possible, they wondered, for a man to actually live like a prince of heaven in the midst of a culture full of perverts, slobs, rebels, and reprobates? Or was it just a nice-sounding ideal that doesn't really work in everyday life? But as Eric and these men explored the pattern of Scripture, it became obvious that God intends His men to exude a superhuman strength, power, purity, and nobility in the midst of a crooked and depraved world. Not only does He provide the vision and command for such a standard, He also provides the strength and power to live it out.

Living by heaven's code of honor isn't just a masculine quality. God has a sacred code of honor for femininity as well. Becoming a woman of honor is the secret to being a woman of sacred feminine mystique. Just as we long for a noble modern-day prince who lives by a heavenly code of honor, godly men long for a noble modern-day princess who carries herself with a royal bearing in all circumstances.

When you prepare to add the quality of feminine mystery to your life, it's important not to limit it to merely relating to the opposite sex or dressing more modestly. Becoming a woman of feminine mystique means becoming a woman of sacred honor in every sphere of life. It's an overall transformation of your inner being by the Spirit of God. When you truly become a handmaiden of the Lord, feminine mystery is a natural by-product. Let's take a look at the specific qualities that mark a woman of honor.

She Is Dead to Self-Interest

A woman of honor must first die before she can live. Christ must become her all in all, even above her desires for romance, love, marriage, family, career, ministry, or accomplishments. Christ said, "If anyone comes to Me and does not hate his father and mother, wife and children, brothers and sisters, yes, and his own life also, he cannot be My disciple" (Luke 14:26).

A woman of honor is like Mary of Bethany, who willing lays down her most sacred and priceless blessings upon the altar before God. She does not cling to her own rights but empties herself in order that Christ's purposes might be accomplished. Amy Carmichael said it well:

> There is no gain except by loss
> There is no life except by death
> Nor glory but by bearing shame
> And that eternal passion says,
> "Be emptied of glory and right and name."[2]

She Is Confident in Christ

A woman of honor must be sure in her step because she knows her Commander. She knows that her King is faithful in all things, and He can be trusted implicitly. Instead of worrying, fretting, or manipulating, she prays and waits for the Lord, knowing He will provide all things needed for life and godliness. She does not need to labor to become self-confident because all her confidence is found in Christ alone.

She Is Valiant

Proverbs 31 portrays the mighty strength of a true woman of honor. "Who can find a virtuous woman?" (verse 10 KJV). The word *virtuous* here is actually a masculine noun that means "strength, might, valor, and power." A woman of honor is a mighty, valiant, valorous woman full of strength and conquering power. She has superhuman strength, because her strength comes from God. She has unmatched valor. She valiantly stomps out whatever stands in the way of God's purposes. Nothing hinders her. Her life is a living display of triumph, victory, and the glory of God.

She Is a Rescuer of the Weak

A woman of honor must be willing to fight on behalf of the weak and the oppressed, willing to give up security and comforts in order to fight her King's battles. She reaches out her hands to the poor and stretches out her hands to the needy (Proverbs 31:20).

Amy Carmichael rescued more than 1000 children from being sold into temple prostitution, and she raised each of them up in the fear and admonition of the Lord. Gladys Aylward led 200 children on a perilous six-week journey to safety in the middle of a war, and she single-handedly stopped a bloody riot at a men's prison. Catherine Booth boldly went into the slums and called the wayward and drunkards to repentance. Jackie Pullinger lived among gang members and prostitutes at risk of her own safety. This is what it means to fight battles on behalf of our King.

She Is an Upholder of Decorum

A woman of honor must not gossip, slander, backstab, criticize, or complain. Her speech must be gracious and respectful at all times. She must not take pleasure in worldly crudeness and humor or in cutting others down. She must always represent her King's glory and nature in the words she speaks.

She Is Harnessed of Soul

A woman of honor is single minded in priority and undeterred by the charm of sexuality, the enticement of alcohol, or the allure of worldly wealth. She must be unavailable to the lusts of flesh, closed to the invitation of compromise, clear minded and strong of presence at all times. The temptations of the world mustn't be looked at, listened to, or entertained even for the slightest moment. She must not take pleasure in evil, but rejoice in the truth.

She Is Unable to Violate Her Conscience

A woman of honor holds her conscience sacred. Her word is her bond, her unbreakable covenant. She does not lie. She does not manipulate. She does not control others. She is a woman of sterling integrity. Others can rely upon her implicitly. Both her earthly and heavenly husband have "full confidence" in her (Proverbs 31:11 NIV). She does not transgress her conscience for any price.

She Is Marked by Purity and Virtue

A woman of honor must demonstrate the regal disposition of heaven. She garners respect with the purity and uprightness of her life. And she must be willing to rebuke those, even of her closest fellowship, that veer from the narrow path of the cross. She must be quick to forgive and unwilling to retain a grudge.

She Is Unafraid of Death

A woman of honor is ready to let go of her earthly life for the sake of her King. Like Vibia Perpetua, who perished in the Roman arena at the age of 19 as an early Christian martyr, she must not count her life dear unto herself but gladly spill it out for the sake of the One who gave everything to her.

She Is a Slave to None but Christ

A woman of honor is never beneath the thumb of man's tyranny. She is not a slave to the lusts of the flesh, the approval of the world, or the pressures of pop culture. If she suffers bodily imprisonment for her belief in Christ, her soul cannot be touched or imprisoned.

She Is Untouched by the World's Opinion

A woman of honor refuses praise and adulation, but rather deflects it heavenward. She does not claim the glory rightfully due her heavenly King. She does not heed either praise or blame, but looks only to the opinion of the Almighty. A woman of honor finds her confidence in the smile of God and from no mere human countenance.

She Possesses Great Inner Stability

A woman of honor must possess a stable core. She feels emotion at great levels, but she is not a slave to her feelings. A woman of honor is of sound mind and does not fall apart emotionally, even in the gravest and most severe of circumstances.

To live as a woman of honor is to be a woman of mystery. A woman who exudes a royal bearing, protects the sacred core of her femininity, and displays the regal character of Christ at all times, will be fascinating, captivating, and riveting to all who behold her. Some may scorn her and label her code of honor "extreme and unnecessary," but those who truly know and love their King will be refreshed and inspired by a woman who protects what is sacred. Remember, we are not expected to live out this high calling in our own strength. The only way it is possible to truly become a woman of honor is to yield our entire lives to the Lordship of Jesus Christ and allow His Spirit to transform every facet of our existence after His pattern. If our heart is willing and we come to Him holding nothing back, He is ready and able to transform us into royalty.

> The royal daughter is all glorious within the palace; her clothing is woven with gold. She shall be brought to the King in robes of many colors; the virgins, her companions who follow her, shall be brought to You. With gladness and rejoicing they shall be brought; they shall enter the King's palace (Psalm 45:13-15).

THE SECRETS OF SACRED LIVING

Showcasing Feminine Mystique in Everyday Life

> *To the pure all things are pure, but to those who*
> *are defiled and unbelieving nothing is pure; but*
> *even their mind and conscience are defiled.*
>
> TITUS 1:15

Not long after I surrendered my life to Christ, I received a hope chest. It wasn't anything fancy; just a small wooden bench that was meant to store special things for my wedding, future home, etc. But for all its simplicity, that hope chest turned out to be one of the best gifts I ever received. Right around the time I began to experience true intimacy with Christ, life took on a brand-new sparkle and freshness. For the first time, I began to notice and cherish sacred things.

While I had been living for selfish pleasure and falling prey to pop culture attractions, the word *sacred* hadn't really been part of my vocabulary.

Centering my life around popularity, pleasure, and the approval of the opposite sex had reduced everything in my existence to something worldly, sensual, and base.

But now that Christ had become the center of my life, He began to train me in the art of sacred living. I began to place a high value on special and meaningful things. My hope chest became a storehouse of sacred treasures. In it I kept journals that chronicled my intimate journey with Christ, poems and songs that had flowed out of my times of private worship, letters to my future husband, promises I felt God had given me, and special notes or sentimental gifts from my family members. Frequently, I would look through my chest, cherishing all the things that had become sacred in my life—my intimate fellowship with Him, my commitment to my future husband, my relationship with my parents and siblings. Once I began to value and cherish sacred things, life was full of beauty and richness like never before.

Eric came into my life right around that same time. Observing his relationship with Christ illustrated to me at a whole new level what it meant to bring the sacred into my daily walk with my King. Eric didn't treat his relationship with God carelessly or take it lightly; rather, he cherished his private times of communion with his Lord above everything else in his life. He viewed his relationship with Christ as the most hallowed honor a person could ever have. This attitude of tender reverence inspired and amazed me. Most young Christians I'd encountered were the opposite—they treated Christ as a casual buddy. Prayer, worship, and intimate fellowship with Him weren't typically valued as a high and sacred privilege by the Christians I'd observed. Rather, spending time with Christ was looked at as more of a duty or obligation.

But Eric's walk with Christ was different. He kept most of the details of his intimate journey with Christ as something sacred and private, not to be shared with others. Even so I was able to gather enough through observation to see that what Eric had with Christ was alive and vibrant, filled with hallowed, significant moments that dramatically shaped his life. He awoke every morning with a listening ear, fully expecting God to guide him, direct him, speak to him, and place divine appointments in his path. He stole away to be alone with God several times each day. He kept a journal of every intimate detail of what God was doing in his life, and his journal was one of his most prized possessions. Certain days of the year held extra meaning and expectation for him because they marked the anniversary of when he had taken a major step forward in his spiritual life. And inevitably, God would do something significant on the very same date, as if to underscore the value of holding such reminders as important. His fellowship with his King was sacred and precious, and it was truly a sight to behold.

I began to apply some of the principles I'd learned in watching Eric's walk with God. Soon, my relationship with Christ became even deeper and more meaningful—filled with sacred, significant moments that propelled me forward in my intimacy with Him. As I learned to cherish and remember the meaningful things God had done in my life and the important truths He was teaching me, I was able to look back and see evidence of His hand in my life in incredible ways, and it served to greatly strengthen my faith.

When God began to script my love story with Eric, cherishing the sacred moments was what added the beauty and fairy-tale sparkle to our romance. We treated every conversation as significant. We didn't spend time together haphazardly, just hanging out watching movies or talking about shallow, trivial things. In fact, because Eric was away for much of our relationship, we weren't able to spend a huge amount of time together. So each time we had the opportunity to enjoy each other's company, we didn't take it for granted. We talked about meaningful, purposeful things—shared stories of God's faithfulness in our life, talked about His plans for our future together, prayed for the least around the world, studied His Word together, and read inspiring Christian biographies. After spending time together, we would each go home and journal what we felt had been special or significant about the conversation. Eric even gave names to many of our special conversations, like "The Night of the Shooting Star" (because we'd been out for a walk and seen a shooting star while talking) or "The Talk on the Grassy Knoll" (because we'd been sitting on a picturesque grass-covered hill during one important conversation.) It probably would have sounded ridiculous to anyone on the outside, but these little touches made our entire love story magical rather than mundane.

I still have journals filled with reminders of those sacred moments we shared together. I have meaningful letters we wrote to each other during the formation of our love story. I have poems and songs Eric shared with me at strategic times in our romance. I still keep them in my hope chest. These sacred things are among our most priceless treasures, and I don't regret for one moment our emphasis on making our romance beautiful, no matter how corny or strange it might have seemed to anyone else.

Even to this day Eric and I put a high priority on protecting the sacred things in life. And we've found this practice to be absolutely essential to making everyday life sparkle and glisten with heavenly beauty. People might make fun of us for our dogged determination to keep life sacred and meaningful, but very few people experience the romance of life the way we do, and we wouldn't trade it for anything.

The Art of Sacred Living

Guarding the sacred isn't just something to apply to our love story or our walk with God. Rather, it can shape and influence every aspect of our daily existence. A young woman who has an eye for protecting the sacred learns how to create beauty in her everyday life. A sacred lifestyle is the natural by-product of a woman who is carefully protecting her inner life. Creating beauty in our outward environment is meant to be the outflow of the joy, beauty, and radiance we've cultivated in our inward life.

I'll never forget reading the story of Betsy ten Boom, when she and her sister Corrie were first put into prison for hiding Jews in their home during the Nazi invasion. The prison was filthy, dark, rancid, and overcrowded with despairing, sick, miserable women. Corrie and Betsy were separated into different cells, and Corrie spent many days wondering how Betsy—who loved beauty, flowers, and sunshine—was fairing in such a destitute, ugly place.

Betsy had always had a gift for making things beautiful—for creating beauty all around her, no matter where she was, even on a meager income. But how could a dank prison cell be made into a haven? One day, Corrie had the opportunity to walk by Betsy's cell and took a quick glimpse inside. To her amazement, she saw that somehow the bleak chamber had been transformed into a sacred sanctuary. "Unbelievably, against all logic, the cell was charming," Corrie wrote. "The straw pallets were rolled instead of piled in a heap, standing like little pillars among the walls, each with a lady's hat atop it. A headscarf had somehow been hung on the wall. The contents of several food packages were arranged on a small shelf. Even the coats hanging on their hooks were part of the welcome of that room, each sleeve draped over the shoulder of the coat next to it like a row of dancing children."[1]

The sacred beautiful environment Betsy had miraculously created was simply a reflection of the beauty and sacredness in Betsy's inner life. Even a dismal prison cell could not crush Betsy's radiance and joy because her inward beauty came from Jesus Christ. And that heavenly beauty could not help but spill over into her environment, no matter where she was.

The painter Thomas Kinkade wrote a little coffee table book called *Simpler Times*. It is one of the very best expressions of sacred living Eric and I have ever read. In it, he writes about the simple, meaningful life that he and his wife have chosen for their family. They deliberately say no to the materialism, rush, and frenzy of society and make time for precious memories instead. Here is how he describes his lifestyle:

> [My wife and I] don't surf the Net. We don't follow CNN.
> In fact, we've chosen to keep television out of our house
> entirely. This is not because we are opposed to the medium

of television, but because we are opposed to what television tends to do in our lives. In our experience, television is a thief that robs us of our time together and steals our peace. When we are watching TV, we are not riding our bikes or playing in the yard or having pillow fights with our girls in the living room. Instead, we are soaking up the subtle and not-so-subtle messages that we should want more, more, and more...and sacrifice our peace if necessary to obtain it...

Most of us are so accustomed to overstimulation that peace feels strange to us; it makes us nervous. Simplicity can be an acquired taste, especially in a society that revels in complexity. But what an improvement when we finally begin to feel at home with a simpler way of life. What a surge of energy when we realize that saying no is really a way of saying yes to all we really care about...

When I learn to say a deep, passionate yes to the things that really matter—and no to whatever gets in the way of that yes—then the peace begins to settle onto my life like golden sunlight sifting to a forest floor. And that, I find, is a peace worth fighting for.[2]

Even if you don't have a spouse and family to focus on, there are plenty of sacred dimensions to life worth cherishing and protecting. Your intimate, daily romance with Jesus Christ. Your study of His Word and going deeper in your Christian life. Your commitment to your future husband. Your relationships with family members and close friends. Your ability to do special things for people in your life, to create and preserve precious memories that will last a lifetime. Your willingness and availability for serving those in need. Your ability to cultivate the special gifts God has given in you in order to more effectively serve His kingdom. These are all sacred things worthy of your focus and protection. But as Thomas Kinkade said, when we become sucked into the frenzy of modern culture, sacred things are quickly crowded out of our life.

Betsy ten Boom's life was one of simplicity and beauty long before she entered that prison cell. She was not living at a frenetic pace, chasing after money, pleasure, entertainment, and popularity. Rather, she lived simply and peacefully, joyfully sharing the little she had with people in need, savoring memories with her family, excelling in the art of gracious hospitality, blessing others in the community with thoughtful gifts and practical service, and cultivating her intimate relationship with Jesus Christ. She excelled at the art of sacred living. And it was an art that she continued to practice, even in prison.

A woman who excels at the art of sacred living is truly a woman of beauty and mystery—a woman who values God's priorities in her life.

Let's explore some practical ways you can begin cultivating a sacred lifestyle in your daily existence.

Creating a Sacred Environment

The Proverbs 31 woman "watches over the ways of her household, and does not eat the bread of idleness" (Proverbs 31:24). One of the most important aspects to a sacred lifestyle is the physical environment in which you cultivate your romance with Christ, create memories, and deepen relationships with others. Whether your personal space consists of an entire home or one small corner of a dorm room, the atmosphere you create in your living environment speaks volumes about your inner priorities. Much like the way we dress, I feel that most of us are in need of a bit more class when it comes to our living environments.

If we live in a sloppy, disorganized environment with clothes strewn all over the floor and dishes piled in the sink, we are likely to *feel* chaotic, scattered, and sloppy as we go about our daily tasks. Not only that, but we send the message to anyone who happens to come into our home that they were not important enough for us to take the time to create a pleasant atmosphere for them to enjoy.

In *Authentic Beauty* I wrote about the importance of creating a sacred inner sanctuary with Christ. One of the best ways to do this is to create an *outward* sanctuary for cultivating intimacy with Him—a set-apart retreat in which you can steal away to deepen your intimate relationship with your Prince. But it's hard to have an amazing prayer time with the TV blaring or the phone ringing. And it's hard to create an intimate retreat for worshipping the King of heaven in a room that smells like dirty laundry and rotten food. Our set-apart sanctuary should be a place that reflects our heartfelt reverence for our heroic Prince—not a sloppy, haphazard environment that showcases laziness and self-focused priorities.

Many of us make our living environment into our own little selfish haven; a place to live and act however we want; to throw our clothes on the floor, indulge in selfish fetishes, or spend time lazily lounging around.

Eric once heard a Christian man make the statement, "You are only as holy as you are in your home." There is no sphere of life that should be outside the radar of God's searchlight, including our home atmosphere. Paul said, "Whether you eat or drink, or whatever you do, do all for the glory of God" (1 Corinthians 10:31). Even the smallest areas of our lives are meant to reflect His glory. Titus 2:5 exhorts women to be "keepers at home" (KJV), which means to govern and watch over household affairs. Governing our home is one of the most basic ways we can cultivate a sacred, God-honoring lifestyle.

Think of your living environment as a tool to serve God's priorities in your life. It's a place to cultivate your romance with Christ. It's a place to deepen relationships with friends and family. It's a place to practice hospitality and bless those in need. It's a place for rest and replenishment rather than selfish indulgence.

Contrary to popular belief, creating a sacred, beautiful home atmosphere is not just for people who have a knack for decorating or who love hanging out at Home Depot. The things in your home are far less important than the attitude in your home. And with a few simple systems and touches, you can transform your little corner or large estate into a beautiful reflection of God's sacred priorities. Here are some thoughts and questions to help get you started:

1. *What type of atmosphere should my living space exude?* Eric and I desire our home atmosphere to be: God-honoring, peaceful, creative, organized, and fun. Describe your ideal home atmosphere in three or four words.

2. *What factors will contribute to this atmosphere?* Some factors that contribute to the atmosphere of our home are: an uncluttered environment, well-organized living and work areas, creative photos and artwork on the walls, and music we enjoy. Make a list of things that could (or currently do) help you achieve *your* desired home atmosphere.

3. *What factors will detract from this atmosphere?* The factors that can easily detract from our peaceful, God-honoring atmosphere are: television, unrestricted phone calls, and messy, disorganized rooms. Make a list of factors that could (or currently do) detract from your desired home atmosphere.

4. *How should other people (family, friends, neighbors) fit into my home environment?* Are there ways in which your home environment could be used to bless others? How can you equip the atmosphere in your living space to be welcoming and refreshing to all who enter? (Eric and I seek to have family and friends in our home regularly, and we even hold some of our ministry retreats at our house so that the people who come feel extra welcomed and connected to us.)

5. *What is God's vision for my quiet time area?* Eric and I each have a place in our house where we go to cultivate our relationship with God. We make sure that there are no distractions in that area of the house (such as the phone or a pile of unfinished work.) We have agreed upon daily

times that each of us will spend our individual time with God, and we don't interrupt each other during those quiet times. We have our journals, Bibles, and study materials easily accessible in our quiet time spot. We have worship music available to listen to in that part of the house. The sacred sanctuary we create for our quiet times makes a world of difference in our ability to cultivate our relationship with God.

What kind of atmosphere will best cultivate your own sacred times of intimacy with Christ? (Worship music, uninterrupted quiet, etc.) Write down a list of things that could (or currently do) help you cultivate a set-apart retreat with Christ. Then write down any practical steps you must take in order to build that kind of atmosphere. (Organize your study materials in that area of the house, purchase a journal and store it in your quiet time spot, have worship music ready to play, etc.)

What kinds of things will detract from your quiet time area? (Television, phone, reminders of work projects, interruptions from roommates or family members, etc.) Write down a list of things that could (or currently do) cause distraction in your quiet times. Then, write down any practical steps you must take in order to remove those distractions. (Unplug the phone, remove the TV, keep reading materials—such as newspapers and magazines—in a different part of the house, etc.)

6. *Do I use my living space for self-focused pleasure or for activities to bring glory to Christ? In what ways?*

7. *Are there things that must be removed from my home in order to make room for God's sacred priorities? (TV, ungodly music, clutter, etc.)*

8. *Have I ever been in a home that truly reflected the beauty of Christ? What were the specific qualities of that environment?*

Once you have gained a clear vision for the kind of home environment you desire, it's time to begin practically creating that environment. If, after answering the questions above, you feel your home environment is already exactly the way it should be, then you probably don't need to read this particular section. But if you are like most young women, there are many practical things that must be done in order to build the right atmosphere for your sacred sanctuary. Here are some practical ways to begin.

Creating Systems

Maybe you've been in the habit of tossing your dirty socks on the floor and leaving them there from the time you were four years old. Even deep-rooted habits can be altered with a little focus and energy.

This is where systems come in. Systems create an ongoing plan for dealing with dirty socks and piles of mail. It isn't enough to simply acknowledge that a stack of mail in your bedroom is a detractor from your sacred time of intimacy with Christ; you must remove the pile of mail and implement a plan to make sure tomorrow's mail doesn't end up in the same place. Your home can only become a sanctuary when all those little areas of life are carefully and purposefully dealt with.

Some say that being organized is a matter of preference or personality rather than necessity. And certainly that is true to a point. To create a sacred sanctuary, you don't have to alphabetize your credit cards or color-code your closet, but taking time to create some basic systems for your living environment will help safeguard your sanctuary from distraction and clutter. Systems prevent dirty socks, piles of old magazines, and stacks of dirty dishes from controlling the atmosphere of your home. Systems protect your home atmosphere against all the little things—from television to junk mail—that can subtly creep in and destroy your sanctuary. So whether you enjoy getting organized or not, remember that the time you spend creating systems is an invaluable investment in your ability to protect the sacred.

Following are some of the most important areas in a modern home environment for which systems must be created. Take time to read through each area and personalize the suggestions to your own situation. If you already have a successful system in place for an area, feel free to skip over it. And if you think of additional systems you need to create for your own specific lifestyle, be sure to write them down and prayerfully explore them.

Your Stuff

The order, peace, and sacredness of your sanctuary will be greatly impacted by the cleanliness of your living environment. It might not seem like a big deal to throw a pile of clothes into the middle of the floor and leave them there for a week, but habits like these will create a sloppy, messy, careless atmosphere. Because your environment is a reflection of your inner priorities, it only makes sense to spend some time focusing on making it an area that truly reflects the beauty, order, and peace of God. Here are some questions to consider:

- What type of atmosphere does your living space currently exude?

- What changes could be made to your living space in order to make it into more of a sacred, Christ-honoring environment?

- Are there areas of disorder that need to be addressed? If so, what are they?

- Would it be helpful to recruit the advice or assistance of a friend or family member to help you develop better cleaning and organization systems?

Can you improve the peace of your home by removing distracting noise and adding beautiful worship music? Can you enhance the beauty of your home by creating a cleaner, more organized atmosphere and getting systems in place for your things? A few small special touches can go a long way in making your living environment a sanctuary.

Even if you don't have a lot of money to work with, there are many creative low-cost or even free ways to build your home into a reflection of beauty—just like Betsy ten Boom did in that prison cell.

The first year Eric and I were married, we had barely enough money to cover the basics, let alone buy extras for our house, but we still desired to make our home a romantic sanctuary. Eric's sister was keeping an old couch and chair in storage. We asked if we could store them in our living room instead. Then we bought an inexpensive slipcover for the couch and put a matching pillow on the chair. Eric had an old trunk from his childhood that contained his stories and drawings from elementary school. We put a runner down the middle of it, set our wedding album on top of it, and made it into a coffee table. We decorated the living room with candles and picture frames we'd been given as wedding gifts. We didn't have a kitchen table, so we covered a card table with a tablecloth and some flowers. We found a couple of old wooden chairs at a garage sale that had character. For about $50 total, we were able to create a wonderful home environment in which to begin building our marriage sanctuary.

If money is an issue, look at what you *do* have to work with and think of ways to use those things creatively. Do you have some old furniture that you could cover or refinish? Can you transform your bedroom by painting the walls a new color? Can you buy some candles to create a peaceful ambiance? Sometimes the challenge of making a great home environment out of odd pieces of this and that can be just as much fun as having a wad of money to spend on new furnishings and decorations.

Your Cell Phone

If you are like most young women, your cell phone is a major part of your daily life. And yet, for all the conveniences it provides regarding staying connected with your friends, your cell phone can easily take on a life of its own. Unchecked, your cell phone can barge in on the peace of your sacred sanctuary and steal away precious time with Christ. It can also inhibit your ability to having a long, uninterrupted conversation with a loved one, having time to read an inspiring Christian biography, or having the energy to help someone in need. Your cell phone should merely be a tool to serve God's priorities in your life. If you ever become a slave to texting or chatting, that's when you know it's time to put some boundaries around your phone use.

Start by determining if there is any time of the day when you need to purposely ignore the phone, such as when you are spending time with friends, helping someone in need, or during your private time of worship and study. If you think hearing the phone ring will compel you to answer it even during the off-limit times, you might need to implement a plan for turning off the ringer or keeping the phone in a different room. Write down the time(s) of day or the specific situations in which you have agreed to not use your cell phone. Write down any action steps you need to take to make your "phone plan" work. Then prayerfully ask God to assist you in making your cell phone a servant to the sacred environment you are working to create.

Your Computer

For most of today's young women, the computer is one of the primary detractors to a sacred, peaceful lifestyle. Social networking, Internet surfing, email, instant messaging, and computer games are just some of the seemingly harmless activities that can quickly strip away your valuable time and undermine the peaceful atmosphere of your sacred sanctuary if proper boundaries aren't created. And then there are the incredible dangers of Internet pornography—poised and ready to entice you with every trip into cyberspace. So if you choose to have a computer and access to the Internet, don't underestimate the significance of creating a careful plan for this area of your life.

Handling Computer Activities

Prayerfully consider what role the computer should play in your home. Will you use it only for email? Will you use it for shopping, and if so, for what kinds of things? What about social networks, computer games, browsing certain websites, visiting certain discussion forums, visiting chat rooms, or instant messaging? Prayerfully consider the specific computer activities you feel are appropriate for your home and sacred sanctuary—keeping in mind the importance of guarding the atmosphere of your home, not to mention your inner life. Write down the specific role the computer will play in your life, and then implement a plan for putting boundaries around it. Defining what your computer is there for will help keep it in its proper place—so that it can be a tool and not a taskmaster in your life.

Handling Computer Time

Time spent on the computer can quickly get out of control. You sit down to briefly check your email or visit your favorite sites, and five minutes suddenly turns into two hours. It is wise to come up with a plan for making sure the computer doesn't rob you of time that should be spent on your true priorities. Prayerfully think through God's highest priorities in your life and then ask yourself these questions: "Is there any time of day when I should make the computer off-limits? Do I need to implement a system for helping keep my computer time in check?" For instance, do you need to set the alarm on your watch when you sit down at the computer so that you don't end up spending more time there than you intended? Do you need to recruit a friend or family member who can help keep you accountable to stay within your allotted time frame? Should you keep your computer in a remote part of the house so you aren't tempted to use up all of your free time in front of the monitor? Write down any action steps you must take in order to implement your "computer time plan."

Guarding Against Internet Dangers

Internet pornography has claimed a prominent place in cyberspace. If you aren't proactive about protecting yourself from Internet porn, it can quickly find its way onto your computer with one careless click of the mouse. The makers of porn sites are relentless in their attempts to lure you at every opportunity. One moment you might be shopping online for space heaters, and the next moment an offensive message flashes in your face. One minute you might be checking your email, the next you are bombarded with explicit photos. Internet pornography is typically far more addictive and dangerous than any other form of its kind because it can be viewed in private, without the shame of having to procure a magazine or video. Allowing any form of this slime into your mind and home environment will immediately destroy the sacredness of your inward *and* outward sanctuary. But there are several things that you can do to protect against this enemy. Be proactive in putting the right barriers in place.

A plan for pop-up porn and offensive spam. There are many resources on the Internet to help you deal with the ever-changing threats of spam and pop-up tactics. You can find programs that control web page content by doing an Internet search such as "Internet content filter." You can also do an Internet search on "How can I stop getting spam?" for additional information. And many online service providers offer "family controls" that filter out adult content. Check with your Internet provider about which of these services they offer, and shop around until you find one that meets your needs. You can also check *www.spamabuse.net*.

A plan for guarding against Internet pornography. You can find helpful information on protecting your home from Internet pornography on websites such as *www.family.org* and *www.nationalcoalition.org*. There is also a service called Covenant Eyes that is designed specifically to keep computer users accountable for the material they look at online. Eric and I use the Covenant Eyes' service. At the end of each month, a list of all the Internet material we individually viewed during the past month is sent to each other's email address. It's a great system. Find out more by visiting *www.covenanteyes.org*.

Prayerfully think through and write down your plan for guarding against offensive material and Internet porn, and any action steps you must take in order to implement this plan.

Be aware that there are many other dangers to cyberspace than online pornography. Recently, I've heard from many Christian young women who admit to being addicted to sites like Facebook and MySpace. A young missionary recently told me that she struggles with spending far more time on Facebook than in prayer or study of God's Word. While these kinds of sites aren't wrong in and of themselves, if we are not watchful over the kinds of things we participate in while using them, or the amount of time we spend on them, they can easily become outlets for gossip, impure interaction with guys, and wasting countless hours on trivial, meaningless topics. If you participate in online networks like these, prayerfully evaluate if they are bearing healthy or unhealthy fruit in your life, and be willing to make radical changes if necessary. Also consider whether online shopping, YouTube videos, or celebrity gossip sites are consuming your time and thoughts in an unhealthy way.

9

EXCELLING AT THE SACRED ART OF HOSPITALITY

Showcasing Christlike Love in Everyday Life

> *Do not let a widow under sixty years old be taken into the number,
> and not unless she has been the wife of one man, well reported
> for good works: if she has brought up children, if she has lodged
> strangers, if she has washed the saints' feet, if she has relieved
> the afflicted, if she has diligently followed every good work.*
>
> 1 TIMOTHY 5:9-10

> *Use hospitality one to another without grudging.*
>
> 1 PETER 4:9 KJV

*T*rue hospitality is a sacred art. It is the act of sharing what you have with others, opening your home to friends and people in need, and blessing them with refreshment and love. Just like etiquette, hospitality is a fading ideal in our modern era. Most young women today are so self-focused that the only time they think of being hospitable is when it somehow benefits *them*. But Scripture is clear that true hospitality is not merely having a few friends over every week to hang out and play games or visit. While this might be a good first step, true hospitality is far more than that.

Hospitality is a demonstration of honor, love, and selflessness. It's an act of "washing the saints' feet"—to refresh, uplift, and strengthen other believers in their faith. It's an opportunity to "lodge strangers"—to share your home and resources with those in need of shelter, food, and love. It's a practical way of "relieving the afflicted"—a decision to put selfish wants aside and pour your time, energy, and focus into those who are lonely, discouraged, sick, or struggling.

Earlier, I mentioned the verses in which Jesus says,

> When you give a dinner or a supper, do not ask your friends, your brothers, your relatives, nor rich neighbors, lest they also invite you back, and you be repaid. But when you give a feast, invite the poor, the maimed, the lame, the blind. And you will be blessed, because they cannot repay you; for you shall be repaid at the resurrection of the just (Luke 14:12-14).

Jesus' version of hospitality is quite backward from our modern thinking. Rather than using hospitality as an opportunity to increase our social status or quell our desire for friendship, He says to use it as a chance to reach out to the outcasts of society, the ones no one else deems valuable. While there is certainly scriptural endorsement placed upon inviting close friends and family members to be guests in our home, we shouldn't stop there. Christ says we are to search out those who are lonely, outcast, and poor, bring them into our homes, and treat them as royalty.

I've spoken with countless missionaries who have been guests in the homes of poor people in other cultures. Often the family has nothing but a meager supply of food, but even if they have to sacrifice their own dinner, they will do whatever it takes to serve a meal to their company and treat them with the utmost honor. Such stories put American

Christians to shame. Most of us don't know how to treat *anyone* as more important than ourselves, let alone sacrifice our own food or comforts in order to serve someone we barely know. It's shameful that dirt-poor families around the world can excel at the sacred art of hospitality, and we who have so very much don't understand the first thing about how to treat others as royalty.

Hospitality, much like social grace, is a reflection of true, Christ-shaped femininity. When a young woman's focus is not on herself, but on serving, honoring, and blessing those in need, hospitality is a natural by-product.

My mom grew up in the South. She has an amazing knack for Southern hospitality unlike any other woman I've met. When she receives guests into her home, the environment is peaceful, orderly, and refreshing, with quiet music playing in the background. The table decor is beautiful, with fresh flowers, lovely dishes, candles, and unique seasonal touches. The food is delicious and satisfying, and you always get the feeling that it was especially prepared just for you. And instead of running around distractedly when company shows up, my mom has mastered the art of being prepared by the time her guests arrive so she can enjoy their fellowship instead of stressing over last-minute details. Her seemingly effortless preparations help everyone relax and enjoy themselves to a much greater degree. And whether her guests are close family members or a family of poor refugees, everyone receives the same royal treatment. They always feel special, honored, and valued when they are treated to my mom's marvelous hospitality.

I have not yet quite mastered this level of hospitality in my own home, though I hope to someday. No matter how organized I feel ahead of time, I still find myself rushing around at the last minute, right as people are arriving. And no matter how foolproof my recipes seem, they hardly ever turn out just right. But even when things don't come off perfectly, there is incredible satisfaction in opening my home and welcoming people in—whether they are strangers or close friends. And when we are able to practice hospitality toward people who don't otherwise get invited places, it's even more fulfilling because we realize we are making an eternal impact.

You don't even have to have your own home to excel in the sacred art of hospitality. When I was 16, I received a card that artistically described the spiritual meaning of my name, Leslie: *peaceful meadow*. The definition of a *peaceful meadow* was a place where others could come and find rest and refreshment. I felt God was reminding me, through that simple definition, that my life was meant to be a place of peace and refreshment for others. As I learned to invest in others' lives, listen to their stories, pray with them, and spend time with them, I discovered what it meant to be a meadow where people could be refreshed. As I've grown older, it's my goal to be a peaceful meadow through all I do (my writing, my friendships, my music, my home, etc). To me, that's the sacred art of hospitality in a nutshell.

It's not an art I always excel at. When I am going through extra-busy seasons or feeling stressed, hospitality quickly falls by the wayside. In our American culture, it's all too easy to get caught up in our own little busy world and forget to open our lives, hearts, and homes to others. Time and time again, God's Spirit has gently reminded me that when I make sacred hospitality a priority, I am valuing what He values and honoring Him.

Let's explore some practical ways to begin cultivating this art at a deeper level in your life, starting today.

Share Some Rainbow Sprinkles

Two summers ago when our daughter Harper arrived home from Korea, Eric and I were surprised to find a neighbor at our door with a homemade meal for us. This neighbor was someone we didn't know well, but her practical display of thoughtfulness blessed us with warmth and refreshment, and even to this day I remember how much that meal touched me. I'm always amazed at the way simple acts of kindness can transform a person's entire perspective. It's a principle I've come to know as "rainbow sprinkles."

The rainbow sprinkles idea began one day when my three-year-old son, Hudson, was moping around the house, calling out to anyone who would listen, "I'm feeling creamy! I'm feeling creamy!" Finally I asked him, "You're feeling creamy? What does that mean?" He looked at me patiently and explained, "It means I want ice cream!" Of course! Why didn't I think of that? It was totally obvious, once he spelled it out for me. Normally I don't just give my kids ice cream at the drop of the hat, but how could I resist a little kid who was "feeling creamy"? I took him to the local malt shop, where he eagerly ordered a mint chocolate chip ice cream cone with rainbow-colored sprinkles. The sprinkles, as the malt shop owner insightfully pointed out, are mainly there for the happiness factor. You really can't taste them, but they brighten up the whole ice-cream experience and make you smile.

Since that trip to the malt shop, I've been on the lookout for ways to add rainbow sprinkles to other people's lives. When you come face-to-face with the overwhelming need out there in the world, it can easily make you feel helpless to do anything significant. However, I've found that even small "sprinkles" can make a huge difference in people's lives. Taking time to reach out to a lonely person, making a child feel special, cooking a meal for a sick person, giving an unexpected gift to a busy person, sending a note to a grieving person—all of these seemingly little gestures can bring incredible joy and comfort (and more importantly, an expression of Christ's love) to those around you.

When Eric and his brother were in missionary school, they would get care packages from home filled with cookies and other treats. They were living on very little food (the school received its food from the local food bank), and so homemade baked goods were a rare luxury. But God was teaching them about self-sacrifice, even in small ways. So instead of eating them, they would wrap them up in gift bags and go around the campus, looking for people to bless. Usually it was just a couple of chocolate chip cookies wrapped up in a bow, but it was amazing to see how such a little thing made such a big impact—it even brought a few people to tears.

I'm all for changing the world and doing "big" things for the kingdom of God—it's what Eric and I are all about. But I never want to forget the small, everyday sprinkles I can use to bless others with. Jesus said, "He who is faithful in a very little thing is faithful also in much" (Luke 16:10 NASB).

Prayerfully consider some small, simple ways you can begin to show thoughtfulness to people in your life. Can you send a card to a discouraged friend? Invite a lonely person out to coffee? Visit a local nursing home and spend time with the patients? Think about the unique gifts and talents God has given you, and consider using these gifts to bless others in creative ways. If you excel at cooking, whom can you serve with that gift? If you have musical talent, how can you share that blessing with those in need?

Many young women I've talked with have found it helpful to plan thoughtful acts into their weeks—making it a goal never to let a week go by without doing at least one thoughtful thing for someone. However you choose to build rainbow sprinkles into your life, you can be sure that as you begin to put this principle into practice, you will experience the joy of sacred hospitality—even if you don't have a home to invite people to!

Become a Peaceful Meadow

I wrote earlier about excelling at the art of good conversation; smiling at people, remembering names, and asking insightful questions. Becoming a peaceful meadow—a person who brings life, rest, and refreshment to the souls of others—takes this principle even further. It's not just being socially sensitive and outward focused. It's becoming the kind of person others can lean on, trust, and draw strength from. We all know what it feels like to be disappointed, let down, or even betrayed by people we trusted. But what amazing joy to find a friend we can trust with our very life; a friend so loyal and Christlike that she would lay down her very life for us. Such friends are rare indeed. But this is the kind of friend Christ has called us to be. "Greater love has no one than this," He said, "than to lay down one's life for his friends" (John 15:13).

A few years ago Eric received a birthday card from a good friend. His friend was reminiscing about the many ways Eric had blessed and refreshed his life. "When I had a serious back injury and had to go in for an MRI," he wrote, "all my other friends said, 'I'll be praying for you.' But you, Eric, went the extra mile. You showed up at the hospital at 5:30 in the morning and stayed there until the whole thing was done, praying and offering me emotional support. I'll never forget that. You've always been the kind of friend who put action to your love."

Becoming a peaceful meadow is going the extra mile in friendship. It's putting your own comforts and agenda aside in order to be there for someone—even if it means losing sleep or not getting as much work done. It's laying down our life for our friends. Amy Carmichael once wrote a "code of honor" for the way Christ had called her to live and act toward her friends and fellow workers. When she evaluated her attitudes and action in light of Christ's "Calvary love" of selflessness and sacrifice, it painted a vivid picture of the way she was to live:

> If I can enjoy a joke at the expense of another; if I can in any way slight another in conversation, or even in thought, then I know nothing of Calvary love...

> If I am afraid to speak the truth, lest I lose affection; if I put my own good name before the other's highest good, then I know nothing of Calvary love...

> If I take offense easily, if I am content to continue in a cool unfriendliness, though friendship be possible, then I know nothing of Calvary love...

> If the praise of others elates me and their blame depresses me; if I cannot rest under misunderstanding without defending myself; if I love to be loved more than to love, to be

served more than to serve, then I know nothing of Calvary love...[1]

I have adopted this same code of honor for my conduct among both
friends and strangers. I do not always excel in each of these points, but
by God's grace it is my goal to become more and more of a peaceful
meadow for others with every passing year of my life.

Prayerfully consider what practical changes you can make in your
life in order to go the extra mile for people. Are you the kind of friend
who can be implicitly trusted, or do you tend to give away secrets,
criticize, and gossip? Are you the kind of person who people know
they can come to, day or night, and receive strength, encouragement,
and unwavering support, or are you too focused on your own needs
and problems to truly be available at that level? Do people receive rest,
refreshment, and godly edification from being in your presence, or
do you merely turn their attention and focus toward shallow things?
Take some time to stack your conduct up against the code of honor
above, and then ask God's Spirit to gently strengthen and refine you
in any areas that are weak.

Being a peaceful meadow ensures you will excel at the sacred art of
hospitality, even if you are in a filthy prison cell. As Christ said, "Come
to Me, all you who are weary and heavy-laden, and I will give you rest"
(Matthew 11:28 NASB). Can we say the same about our own life?

Creating a Welcoming Home

As we learn to add the rainbow sprinkles and peaceful meadow
principles to our inner lives, it only stands to reason that our outward
environments would become a reflection of caring, welcoming, and
warmth as well. If you are blessed with your own living space (even
if it's just a tiny dorm room), you have a great opportunity to create
a welcoming, loving atmosphere in which others can come and enjoy
peace, rest, and refreshment.

I remember visiting a missionary training college where two young women were living in a small hotel-style room on the campus. Rather than keeping their room cold and impersonal, they added some simple touches and transformed their room into a restful haven for all who entered. They placed a cozy rocking chair in one corner. They positioned a vase with fresh flowers on the dresser. They added some handmade pillows to their beds. And they hung their favorite photos in frames on the wall. Everyone who came into their "home" felt welcomed and refreshed, and they quickly forgot they were sitting in a cramped room on a college campus.

Just like Betsy ten Boom in the prison cell, creating warmth and beauty in our outward environment should be the outflow of our inner life—and it's something we can do even if we are sitting in a dirty prison cell.

Thomas Kinkade writes about the "glow in the windows" that he adds to nearly all his paintings of homes and cottages. It's a glow that comes from a home full of laughter, love, and warmth. He says:

> In our house, we know each other. We talk a lot. We know where each other is ticklish. We read together from children's books or from our big family Bible. We paint together... We play games in our house...We sing songs—making up in enthusiasm what we lack in talent. We also love to bring friends into the warm circle of light in our home... Sometimes we play board games...or take a walk around the neighborhood. Mostly though, we sit and talk...about books, old movies, about hopes and dreams, about the many blessings God has given us...That kind of conversation has almost become a lost art in our high-tech age...Here in America, we've installed television sets everywhere so that people never have to converse...Have you ever walked at night by a window where the television was on? The light is dim and cold. But walk at night by a window where a fire is flickering, where a candle is lit, and see the difference. The

warm glow in the windows is so inviting that it draws you in. It's not high-tech entertainment that puts warmth in the windows, but human connection. It's human warmth that makes up the golden glow.[2]

What are some ways you can add that kind of glow to the windows of your own home, in order to bless and refresh others? Candles, music, homemade meals, fresh-baked cookies, flowers, and warm decorations can go a long, long way in adding that cozy, welcoming light to your home. But it's even more important to consider the activities and attitudes that take place when you invite people over. Do you cultivate meaningful conversation? Do you sit and really listen as they share their heart? Do you laugh and enjoy each other's company without having to rely on high-tech entertainment to do so? Do you turn the focus toward things of heaven? Do people come away from your home feeling as though they encountered Christ?

Allow God to mold and refine this area of your life. As you think and pray about making the atmosphere of your home more welcoming, you may find it helpful to write down practical and creative ideas that come to mind. Creating your own special glow in the windows of your home is one of the most fun and enjoyable aspects of God-centered hospitality!

10

AWAKENING TO THE ROMANCE OF LIFE

Cherishing the Adventure of Each Day

*Contrary to popular opinion, romance is not a relationship—
although it can add fullness and spice and excitement to a
connection between two people. Romance is not heart and
flowers and violins, although an evening of hearts and flowers
and strings can be soaringly romantic. Romance is instead
an attitude, a set of habits, a way of encountering the world.
You are a romantic when savoring experience is a priority
for you, when you are willing to invest time and energy
into making your experiences more vivid and memorable.*

THOMAS KINKADE

*E*ric has often described himself as a hopeless, incurable romantic.
Often what people assume by that statement is that his life revolves
around love letters, candlelight, romantic sonnets, and a dozen red
roses. But that's not exactly true. Granted, Eric is attuned, far more

than most guys, to fueling the romantic fire in our marriage—much to my delight. However, his romantic qualities go far beyond the realm of human romance. Eric loves life. He has a passion for living, an excitement to be alive each day, a hunger to experience the fullness of all God has for him on this earth. He savors the romance and adventure of living a Christ-scripted life. He deliberately adds a zest to life wherever he goes, whatever his circumstances. He excels at enjoying the romance of life probably better than anyone else I've ever met. And in the 17 years I've known him, I've become somewhat of a hopeless incurable romantic too—caught up in the epic adventure of a God-centered life. It's a most exciting way to live.

Eric and I believe God doesn't merely intend for life on this earth to be endured; rather, He intends life to be *savored*—every experience can be purposeful, meaningful, and significant. Every day is an opportunity to discover more of Him.

Even when we are going through something challenging, we like to imagine dramatic movie score music playing in the background of our life—reminding us that even trials are exciting God-given opportunities to gain greater victory, patience, faith, strength, and dependence upon Him.

Those who excel at the art of sacred living know how to savor the romance of life. It doesn't happen by adopting a self-focused, short-term, pleasure-seeking attitude, but by learning how to cherish and value the opportunities God gives us in each day. Daily life is bursting with opportunities to enjoy His amazing creation; opportunities to cultivate relationships with family and friends; opportunities to build God's kingdom; opportunities to create, to sing, to dance, to worship, to serve, to laugh, and to learn. And those who have awakened to the romance of life are great at noticing and maximizing these moments.

For example, there are two different ways I can approach dinner with my family. If I hastily whip up some instant macaroni and cheese and plop it down on the table without any placemats, our family tends to eat mechanically and quickly move on to the next thing without really enjoying the meal together. Alternatively, if I put just a little time and energy into setting the table, lighting some candles, turning on some music, and making a more thoughtful dinner, our family lingers at the table, talking, laughing, and savoring the opportunity to slow down and be together after a busy day. The first approach might be functional, but it is hopelessly unromantic. The second is fun, fresh, and vibrantly romantic.

There are two ways I can approach a book deadline. If I keep my sweats on and sit alone in a disheveled, disorganized office, scowling at my computer screen for hours, I tend to loathe the entire project by the time it is finished. But if I dress nicely, organize my desk, turn on some soft music, and put a cup of hot tea by my computer, the whole experience changes. Suddenly, it becomes fun, even romantic, to accomplish a project. By savoring and enjoying the experience, I come away feeling fulfilled rather than drained.

The same goes for just about every area of life. As Betsy ten Boom displayed, even a prison cell can be approached with beauty and romance, with a bit of creativity and a Christ-centered attitude. I certainly don't always excel at savoring and maximizing opportunities for romance in my daily life (we still have some nights where we eat mac and cheese in plastic bowls), but I make it my focus to excel in this area more and more with each passing year.

The more we awaken to the romance of life, the more sacred and meaningful life becomes.

Here are a few practical ways to begin incorporating a romantic attitude into your daily life.

Create Memorials

One of the main things that helps to keep my romance with Christ so alive and vibrant is taking the time to create memorials of my journey with Him—a skill I learned from Eric back when he first came into my life. For me, keeping a journal has become an amazing way to remember and document the incredible things God is doing in my life. I write down Scriptures that touch my heart, specific answers to prayer, and promises I feel He's given me. Chronicling the significant moments in my walk with God creates a memorial of His faithfulness to me and greatly strengthens my faith and trust in Him as I grow and face new challenges. I still have the journals I kept during my blossoming romance with Eric. What an invaluable treasure to look back at them and be reminded of the special conversations we had, the beautiful promises God whispered to my heart, and the amazing ways in which He scripted our love story.

Another way I create memorials in my relationship with God is to write songs about specific things He's teaching me, or significant experiences I have in my walk with Him. Sometimes the songs are good enough to share with others, but even if they are not, it doesn't matter—they help to commemorate something precious and mean-ingful in my spiritual life. Singing them, even years later, reminds me once again of the faithfulness of my God. Eric and I love to write songs together (something we did a lot of during the early days of our friendship) about the amazing truths we discovered in God's Word. We still have them in a special notebook and we love to go back and sing them—they remind us of the fire and passion that filled our spirits when we learned an important spiritual truth for the very first time.

Christ cautions us in Revelation 2:4 against forsaking "our first love." One of the best ways to keep our love story with our heavenly Prince fresh and alive is to *remember* and *cherish* His fingerprints upon our life story. Amy Carmichael often wrote poems about significant things her Lord taught her. Keith Green wrote songs to commemorate God's work in His life. Reese Howells offered God "thank offerings" for spiritual victories by giving something of significance to someone in need.

Consider some ways you can begin to cherish the significant moments in your walk with Christ. Even if they are only small things no one else would appreciate, remember that this is something special between you and the Lover of your soul. Begin asking yourself how you can create memorials whenever He does something important in your life. A friend of mine often makes an artistic collage to memorialize God's work in her life. Another friend takes beautiful black-and-white photos and frames them—sometimes with an important Scripture verse scripted over the picture. Whether you choose to journal, write a poem or song, paint a masterpiece, or do something else that is unique to you, taking the time to commemorate the "God moments" of life will add sparkle, romance, and beauty to your spiritual journey—and keep your first love fresh and alive.

Creating memorials in other areas of life can have the same effect. Quite a few years ago, when Eric and I were in the midst of a whirlwind season of nonstop travel, we began to realize that we weren't remembering much about our life. We were in so many cities that every trip seemed to blur together. We met so many people that we never retained anyone's name or personal story. We decided something needed to change. We bought a digital camera and began taking pictures to remember our daily life. We took pictures of coffee shops we visited, people we met on the road, one of us holding up a newly completed book manuscript, weddings we attended, and even funny signs we saw while driving across the country.

Not long after getting the camera, we started a tradition called "Scraps." Every couple of weeks, we'd create a new page or two in a photo album, pasting in pictures of our daily life, writing down funny things that had happened to us, even chronicling favorite new songs, books, or foods we'd tried.

As we looked back over our Scraps, life suddenly didn't seem like such a blur. Rather, we chuckled with fondness at the memories we'd preserved. Scraps became a wonderful way to savor life rather than merely enduring it.

We've continued the Scraps tradition for quite some time and greatly improved it over the years. Our house is filled with artistic photos of our family, our kids, and our loved ones, daily reminding us of the many incredible blessings God has given us. We don't just hang formal, posed pictures up in our house. We prefer to capture the humor and drama of daily life in our family photos. On our dining room wall there is a large photo of three-year-old Hudson's first encounter with a life-sized Pluto at Disneyland. The camera caught him just as he was looking up at the big dog and bursting into tears of bewilderment. It's a hilarious picture, and it makes all of us laugh whenever we see it. Photo albums, pictures in frames, and artistically crafted home movies add a warmth, beauty, and romance to our life like nothing else can. It helps us cherish the precious family moments God gives us.

Eric and I also like to create special memorials in our own relationship. Mostly, we do this through letters we write to each other. We take time to thoughtfully capture feelings for each other or memories we've shared and then handwrite or type the letter with a romantic, scripty font onto beautiful, scented stationary. We have entire boxes full of the love letters we've written to each other over the years. Sometimes Eric will write me a song, or I'll write a poem for him and put it in a special frame. Creating memorials in our marriage keeps our romance fresh and beautiful.

Consider some ways in which you can begin creating memorials in your own daily life. You don't have to be married with kids in order to preserve the many precious moments God gives you. Writing letters to special friends, framing photos of significant happenings in your life, creating scrapbooks of your favorite things, or preserving important memories in other creative ways will add romance, sparkle, and beauty to your daily existence in a way that few other things can.

Be All There

Jim Elliot once wrote, "Wherever you are, be all there." In our microwaveable, fast-paced society, most of us are distracted and preoccupied with a hundred different things at any given time. In order to savor the romance of life, we must learn how to live purposefully—to treat each conversation, experience, and activity as valuable and worthy of our time and focus. It means a shift from a haphazard, fly-by-the-seat-of-your-pants lifestyle to thoughtful, meaningful living. It means not carelessly spending our time on mindless, meaningless things, but treating each moment of the day as a valuable gift from God, not to be wasted on selfish whims.

I enjoy an afternoon at the park with my children far more when I pour all my energy into laughing with them, tickling them, and nurturing them than when I am talking on my cell phone and watching them play out of the corner of my eye. My quiet times of prayer and study are far more effective when my mind and emotions are fully focused on Jesus Christ, rather than constantly wandering in all directions or worrying about what I'm going to make for dinner that night.

It's extremely hard to savor the romance of life when our minds and hearts are scattered and preoccupied. Unless we are *all* there, we can't truly notice or appreciate the significant moments God blesses us with.

One of the greatest ways to cut down on mental clutter and distraction in life is to remove (or at least greatly reduce) the amount of technology and high-tech entertainment we so easily allow into our life. Television, movies, and the Internet can quickly steal our focus so that even when we are not engaged in those activities, our mind and subconscious are constantly on overload. I can't count the number of times I've been trying to pray, only to have a scene from a movie begin to replay in my head, pulling my focus away from heavenly things and back onto earthly things.

I wrote in my book *Set-Apart Femininity* about the major lifestyle shift that Eric and I have chosen in the area of movies and entertainment. In the past few years, we've basically cut out all movies and television from our life and have given our free time to prayer and deepening our relationship with Christ and each other. It may sound like drudgery, but it's been like a breath of fresh air to our souls. It's added far more romance and beauty to our life than any fancy home theater with surround sound ever could. Removing my unhealthy dependence on Hollywood's short-term pleasure has freed me to savor the *true* pleasures of life—riding our bikes to the local malt shop with our kids, having a picnic by the lake, baking a special dessert just for fun, making creative gifts for friends and neighbors, planting flowers in the spring, building a snowman and then drinking hot chocolate in the winter, and having lively game nights with family or friends. Not to mention freeing my mind to be far more present, alert, and focused during conversations and prayer times.

Begin to prayerfully consider ways that you can cut out distracting things from your life and free your heart and mind to be *all* there, wherever you are. How can you replace mindless entertainment with healthy, beautiful, relationship-building, romantic pastimes? Opportunities for romance abound every day, but often we must quiet the clamor of the world in order to see them.

11

NOBLE BEAUTY

The Refreshing Radiance of a Forgiving Woman

> *Be kind to one another, tenderhearted, forgiving*
> *one another, even as God in Christ forgave you.*
>
> EPHESIANS 4:32

*H*er name was Dolly. Dolly was eighty-seven years old, and she was beautiful. Nearly blind and in frail health, she was confined to a nursing home and spent most of her days sitting in a wheelchair, knitting scarves for her great-grandchildren or playing checkers with the nurses. When I was sixteen, my brothers and I went to see her during our weekly visits to the nursing home. Every week, we would knock on Dolly's door and she would light up with a genuine smile. "It's so wonderful to see you!" she would exclaim as she joyfully held out her hands in welcome. Though Dolly's body was wasting away, her mind was sharp. She was funny and witty, and she loved to be told good jokes or interesting trivia. Dolly enjoyed talking about God, and she especially loved to hear my brothers and me sing worship songs. She was by far our favorite patient in the nursing home, and we lingered in her room longer than any other. Her joy was contagious. She had sparkling eyes, silky white hair, and rosy cheeks. It was clear Dolly had lived a rich, full life and that she did not have many, if any, regrets. I think that was what made Dolly stand out so dramatically from the rest of the patients.

So many of the older men and women we encountered seemed to be wallowing in regret, heartache, and bitterness. One woman, named Simone, had once been a fashion model. On her dresser was a framed glamour shot of herself from younger days, beautiful and seductive. But now in her old age nothing was left of her beauty. She was hardened and bitter. Every time we talked with her, she was complaining, griping, or criticizing. It was clear her life had been quite a disappointment, and that for all the favor and beauty she used to possess, they did not provide lasting happiness.

Dolly had settled all her accounts. There was no one in her past she was bitter toward, and she enjoyed the last years of her life to their fullest. Simone, on the other hand, carried many painful wounds that had never been healed. She was angry and resentful toward just about everyone, from her son, who had placed her in the nursing home, to her husband, who had died five years ago, to the nurse who forgot to bring her the right blanket.

It was stunning to see the difference in beauty between the two women. Dolly glowed with life and radiance, while Simone, the former model, wasted away in bitterness and ugliness. It's a lesson I've never forgotten.

Not only is being gracious and forgiving the pattern of the Gospel, it's a crucial element to true feminine beauty; the kind of beauty that will last long after physical allure has faded.

Bitterness, resentment, and unforgiveness can turn even the most physically beautiful woman into a hard, cold, undesirable, unattractive female. But by the same token, graciousness, forgiveness, and guileless-ness can transform a physically plain woman into a radiant princess. Just think about women you have met who are seething with anger and bitterness. Are they pretty and ladylike or rigid and ugly? God's Word says it is "better to dwell in the wilderness, than with a conten-tious and angry woman" (Proverbs 21:19). An angry, bitter, unforgiving woman is one of the most undesirable kinds of people in the world.

As women, it's too easy to be quick tempered, to be ruled by our feelings and emotions rather than by the Spirit of God. When some-one hurts us, our natural, fleshly side wants to cling to that hurt, to meditate upon it, and to hold that person in contention for the rest of his or her life. When someone offends us, our feminine tendency is to pout, sulk, and act moody and sullen to send the message that they have really messed up—or to say critical and cutting things about them to others. For some reason, our flesh convinces us that being bitter toward those who hurt us is our God-given right. But the opposite is true. Christ spoke in no uncertain terms about the neces-sity of forgiving:

> Then Peter came to Him and said, "Lord, how often shall my brother sin against me, and I forgive him? Up to seven times?" Jesus said to him, "I do not say to you, up to seven times, but up to seventy times seven. Therefore the kingdom of heaven is like a certain king who wanted to settle accounts with his servants. And when he had begun to settle accounts, one was brought to him who owed him ten thousand tal-ents. But as he was not able to pay, his master commanded that he be sold, with his wife and children and all that he had, and that payment be made. The servant therefore fell down before him, saying, 'Master, have patience with me, and I will pay you all.' Then the master of that servant was moved with compassion, released him, and forgave him the debt. But that servant went out and found one of his fellow servants who owed him a hundred denarii; and he laid hands

on him and took him by the throat, saying, 'Pay me what you owe!' So his fellow servant fell down at his feet and begged him, saying, 'Have patience with me, and I will pay you all.' And he would not, but went and threw him into prison till he should pay the debt. So when his fellow servants saw what had been done, they were very grieved, and came and told their master all that had been done. Then his master, after he had called him, said to him, 'You wicked servant! I forgave you all that debt because you begged me. Should you not also have had compassion on your fellow servant, just as I had pity on you?' And his master was angry, and delivered him to the torturers until he should pay all that was due to him. So My heavenly Father also will do to you if each of you, from his heart, does not forgive his brother his trespasses" (Matthew 18:21-35).

Forgiveness is an essential part of the Christ-life. It's not optional. We cannot have a vibrant relationship with Jesus Christ if we hold resentment and bitterness in our heart. In fact, Christ goes as far as to say we will not receive forgiveness from our heavenly Father if we do not forgive those who have wronged us.

I am well aware that most girls reading this book have been hurt in deep, significant ways. With sin and selfishness ruling our culture, you more than likely have experienced abuse (sexual, physical, or emotional) or some other kind of severe cruelty during your growing-up years. If you've ever given your heart to a selfish guy, chances are you've experienced the cutting pain of rejection or betrayal. If you've developed friendships with self-focused girls, you've probably been stabbed in the back, lied to, and taken advantage of. And the list goes on.

To be a gracious, forgiving woman is not easy. In fact, it's not even possible without the supernatural enabling power of God's Spirit. But our Lord promises to give us *all* things that we need for life and godliness (2 Peter 1:3), and that includes the power to forgive.

Corrie ten Boom tells a moving story about finding power to forgive someone in a situation when it felt impossible to do so. After enduring unspeakable miseries, including the death of her sister Betsy, in a German concentration camp, Corrie relied on the grace of God to forgive her enemies and become a living testimony of the power of God. She began to travel the world and speak about His amazing grace. One night, after sharing her testimony at a church in Germany, a man approached her. "What you said tonight greatly impacted me," he said sincerely. "I have done many things in my life I deeply regret. What a miracle to know Christ is willing to forgive even me."

As he was speaking, Corrie froze in shock. She recognized him. He had been a guard at the concentration camp where Betsy had lost her life—one of the very cruelest guards. And now he was extending his hand in friendship to her. All of the old emotions—the anger, resentment, and indignation—she had experienced in the camp came flooding back. She found herself unable to take the man's hand or even reply. She felt God challenging her to forgive him, just as she had been forgiven and washed clean by Jesus' blood for her own sins:

> I tried to smile, I struggled to raise my hand. I could not. I felt nothing, not the slightest spark of warmth or charity. And so again I breathed a silent prayer. Jesus, I prayed, I cannot forgive him. Give me Your forgiveness.

"You take the step of obedience," came God's gentle reply, "and I will do the rest."

So Corrie obeyed. She reached out and shook the man's hand. As she did so, the supernatural love of Christ flooded her heart. She saw him as Christ did. And her bitterness was replaced by love and compassion:

> As I took his hand the most incredible thing happened. From my shoulder along my arm and through my hand a current seemed to pass from me to him, while into my heart sprang a love for this stranger that almost overwhelmed

me. And so I discovered that it is not on our forgiveness
any more than on our goodness that the world's healing
hinges, but on His. When He tells us to love our enemies,
He gives, along with the command, the love itself.[1]

Forgiveness is not primarily a matter of feeling, but a matter of
choice; a decision to obey. When we simply say, "Lord, I choose to let
this go, to give this offence to You instead of carrying it," God supplies
the willingness, the love, and the compassion needed to practically live
it out. When it comes to a decision of whether or not to forgive, we
must remember that we ourselves have been forgiven and delivered
from an eternity in hell. We did not deserve Christ's unconditional love,
but He gave it anyway. And He asks us to do the same in return—to
forgive even those who are undeserving.

Being a gracious, forgiving woman does not merely apply to the
major offenses that have happened in our lives, but in the way we
treat people on a daily basis. Every day we encounter rude, insensitive
people. We come across undesirable, sinful people. We rub shoulders
with arrogant, self-focused people. We take the brunt of others' stress.
There are two ways to respond: with nobility or with selfishness.

A woman with noble, gracious, Christlike beauty does not take
offense easily. She is not critical and judgmental toward others. She
doesn't turn down her nose at undesirable people. Rather, she's a reflection of 1 Corinthians 13:

> Love suffers long and is kind; love does not envy; love does
> not parade itself, is not puffed up; does not behave rudely,
> does not seek its own, is not provoked, thinks no evil; does
> not rejoice in iniquity, but rejoices in the truth; bears all
> things, believes all things, hopes all things, endures all things
> (1 Corinthians 13:4-7).

These are not meant to be flowery words on a page. This is a beautiful description of Christlike love in action—a vivid picture of the

way we are called to live and to interact with others on a daily basis. Most of us need to apply some focus and discipline, combined with a deep dependence upon the power of God, in order to become gracious and forgiving in our day-to-day life.

Here are some practical ways to put this nobility into practice, starting today.

Keep Your Accounts Short

Someone once said that your humility can be measured by how quickly you admit you are wrong. Though it is uncomfortable and damaging to your pride, if you ask forgiveness from someone *the moment* you realize you have wronged them, you keep accounts short rather than allowing a case to be built up against you. You honor the other person by showing your relationship with them is even more valuable than your pride. Next time you realize that you have hurt someone, done something insensitive, or been selfish in your attitude, immediately go to them and ask their forgiveness. It may be painful at first, but the more you put this into practice, the more it will become a Christlike habit in your life. You will find that people's love and respect for you only grows when you are willing to humble yourself by quickly admitting your faults.

Similarly, the moment you recognize that someone has hurt you, immediately stop, pray, and give the offense back to God. The more you mull over it, think about it, and go over the scene in your mind, the more it has opportunity to take root within your soul and plant deep seeds of bitterness. But if you are quick to forgive, you keep your heart and conscience clean before God. Even if the other person never comes to you and asks your forgiveness, remember that forgiveness is first and foremost an issue between you and God. We are not to merely forgive only when someone becomes humble and admits their faults, but even when they don't realize what they have done. Remember Jesus on the cross praying, "Father, forgive them; for they know not what they do"? (Luke 23:24). It is not your job to force someone to a place of repentance. That is between them and God. Your only job is to love them as Christ loves you, and to demonstrate His noble love no matter how they act in return.

Don't withhold affection, act aloof and distant, or pout in order to let someone know they have offended you. If it's something that needs to be discussed, go to them in a gentle, respectful manner and speak truthfully about how they have hurt you. (Don't approach them in the heat of anger or emotion, but only once you've already forgiven them in your heart and given the offense to God.) Or, if it's something better left unspoken, pray that God will soften and change their heart in His own perfect time and way. Love and respect others, even when they don't deserve it. If you yield to Him, Christ will offer you the grace and strength you need to keep your own slate clean, irregardless of how messy the other person's slate may be.

Even after 14 years of marriage, Eric and I don't carry around bitterness and resentment toward each other for past hurts. This isn't because we never hurt each other—far from it. Rather, our marriage slate is kept clean because we deal with issues as soon as they arise. It's a conflict habit we developed when we were first married, and it has made an incredible difference in our relationship. Never once have we gone to bed angry with each other—even if it meant we had to stay up all night talking things out and making them right. We kill the seeds of bitterness before they have a chance to grow. We wake up each morning knowing that things are right between us.

Not long ago I bumped into an acquaintance of mine—a young twentysomething woman who had been a Christian for several years. After chatting for a few moments, I began to ask how certain of her friends and family members were doing. "Oh, I am not on speaking terms with that person," she remarked coolly. I asked her about another person. "I don't speak to her anymore, either," she informed me with a careless toss of her head. She had a list of at least five people she was in conflict with—and she appeared to have no interest in mending the relationships. It seemed to give her a sense of control to hold grudges and give people a cold shoulder.

All too many young women fall prey to the short-lived sense of power they find in holding offenses over others, refusing to speak to friends who have hurt them, or gossiping about their faults to everyone they meet. But not only will this attitude cripple our intimate relationship with Christ, as we discussed earlier, it quickly replaces graceful feminine beauty with hardened, ugly bitterness.

Do not allow the seeds of bitterness to grow in your life. Learn to quickly forgive and be easily forgivable, and you will enjoy the blissful freedom of a guileless inner life and you will glow with a beauty that will last the rest of your life, like sweet little old Dolly!

Give a Gentle Answer

Proverbs 15:1 says, "A soft answer turns away wrath, but a harsh word stirs up anger." When someone speaks rudely or says something insensitive to us, the way we respond is critical. Our selfish, fleshly side urges us to respond harshly, insisting that it is our right to be rude to those who are rude to us. But Christ's pattern is completely different. He says,

> You have heard that it was said, 'You shall love your neighbor
> and hate your enemy.' But I say to you, love your enemies,
> bless those who curse you, do good to those who hate you,
> and pray for those who spitefully use you and persecute
> you (Matthew 5:43-44).

There might not be anything more challenging to our flesh than to live out this principle of selflessness, unconditional love, and forgiveness. To bite our tongue when a harsh reply wants to burst out, to take a deep breath and pray for the other person instead. To exude the nature of Christ in the face of rudeness, insensitivity, or cruelty is a supernatural ability that His Spirit gives and not something we can muster up in our own strength.

One of the things that helps me most when it comes to giving a gentle answer is to remember stories of persecuted Christians through-out the ages. Betsy ten Boom was able to see her vicious, murderous prison guards with eyes of compassion instead of hate. Sabina Wurmbrand was able to sincerely love the pastor whose betrayal of her husband caused him years of torture and imprisonment. Elisabeth Elliot was able to forgive and serve her husband's killers. Vibia Perpetua was able to intercede for the salvation of those who tortured and humiliated her before they took her life.

If these women could receive grace and strength to love even the cruelest of men, can we not trust God for the power to overlook the much smaller offenses we encounter every day?

A woman who has been transformed by the selfless love of Christ is not easily angered. She does not fly off the handle. She is not a slave to tumultuous emotions. She is not concerned with protecting her right to be treated a certain way. She is far more interested in the eternal souls of those around her than in her own feelings.

As women, we've often been trained to believe we are slaves to our emotions; that we can't help it when our feelings overcome us, controlling what we say and how we act. But contrary to popular belief, outbursts of anger, tears of self-pity, overwhelming feelings of hurt, and even hormonal ups and downs can all be conquered by God's Spirit overtaking our inner being. His love and life are far more powerful than our most intense emotions. And we are not to be controlled by anything but His Spirit.

If you feel controlled by volatile emotions, pray specifically for God to overtake your emotions and bring them under His jurisdiction. Next time you are in a situation where you feel your emotions flying off the handle, make a decision to slow down, walk in the other room if needed, take a deep breath, and pray for *His* love, *His* attitude, and *His* response to flow through your being. If you silence the voice of your screaming emotions and tune in to the still, small voice of His Spirit, gentle answers will begin to replace angry ones. And soon people will stop and take notice of the unusual grace, beauty, and nobility that emanates from your life. A woman who is free from the tyranny of her own emotions is truly a sight to behold.

Flee Gossip

Gossip is one of the ugliest habits a young woman can allow into her life. It often seems so harmless at first, but gossip is deadly to our spiritual lives and disastrous to our friendships and relationships. In fact, it's one of the main ingredients to bitterness, tension, and ruined relationships. God's Word says, "Gossip separates close friends" (Proverbs 16:28 NIV). Deliberately choosing to avoid gossip can quell even the most intense conflicts. As Proverbs 26:20 says, "Without wood a fire goes out; without gossip a quarrel dies down" (NIV).

When God first began to purify the inner terrain of my soul, gossip was one of the first areas He convicted me of. Though it had not been my habit to maliciously gossip about people, I hadn't seen any harm in engaging in a little lighthearted banter about someone's annoying social habits or irritating quirks. It was the kind of conversation that usually began with someone saying, "Not to be mean or anything, because I really like so-and-so, but have you ever noticed how they always do such-and-such?" Because this kind of conversation often took place among church friends, I had somehow felt it was justified. Yet I finally realized that this pattern did not reflect the likeness of Jesus Christ. It did not enhance His beauty in my life. It only fueled my fleshly, self-ish side. By His grace, I determined not to participate in or even listen to *any* form of gossip, no matter how innocent it seemed.

As I am writing this, I'm sitting in a coffee shop, not far from a table where an outspoken Christian young woman is catching up with one of her best friends and talking in a loud voice that's impossible to ignore. For the past half hour, she's been talking about her desire to be serious about God and live a life of true surrender to Him. But within the past few minutes, she's been speaking reproachfully about a mutual friend she is "concerned about." "Julie has been acting so weird," she is saying in a voice of disgust. "I don't know what her problem is. She totally needs God to straighten her out. You wouldn't believe what she did the other day…" And then she launches into a detailed, juicy account of all Julie's "problems" and recent offenses. "I guess she needs prayer or something. I'm just so sick of being around her," she concludes. Her voice is anything but compassionate, and she is certainly not displaying an attitude of prayerful concern. This is Christian gossip at its worst; spiritual-sounding criticism that is actually more about tearing someone down rather than fighting for God's best in their life.

As I listen to this girl talk, I can't help but notice once again how unattractive gossip is in a young woman. It's the opposite of Christlike nobility. It's completely unfitting for a set-apart daughter of the King.

In 2 Corinthians 12:20 (NIV), Paul writes about his concern over one of the churches:

> I am afraid that when I come I may not find you as I want you to be…I fear that there may be quarreling, jealousy, outbursts of anger, factions, slander, gossip, arrogance and disorder.

Just think about how perfectly this describes the state of affairs in a typical sorority house, girls' dorm, or clique of high school girlfriends. Young women can be masterful at the art of gossip, backstabbing, arrogance, conflict, and betrayal. Christian young women are often no exception. Paul rebukes idle, slanderous, gossipy young women in 1 Timothy 5:13 (NASB):

> At the same time they also learn to be idle, as they go around from house to house; and not merely idle, but also gossips and busybodies, talking about things not proper to mention.

Gossip is not something to take lightly. It's destructive, ugly, and damaging to friendships and relationships. It must be ruthlessly purged from our lives. Prayerfully evaluate this area of your life before God. Here are some questions to ask:

- Do I use gossip as a weapon to get back at those who have hurt me?

- Do I gossip under the seemingly spiritual banner of being "concerned" about people?

- Do I use my tongue to honor and build up, or tear down and criticize?

- When someone offends me, am I quick to report it to others?

Ask God to purge any patterns of gossip from your life. Next time you feel the urge to speak words of criticism or gossip, ask God's Spirit to take over your tongue. Pray for the person you are tempted to gossip about. And let God deal with their "issues" instead of you.

Important side note: Keep in mind that it's also possible to gossip through corporate prayer. Over the years I've noticed many Christian young women praying in group settings, mentioning all the things they were concerned about in someone's life, and drawing every listener's attention to that person's weaknesses. Since it comes in the form of a prayer, it often doesn't seem like gossip. But prayer that publicly broadcasts sin, weakness, offenses, or indiscretions in a person's life is not edifying but destructive. If you desire to take your concerns over someone's life to God in prayer, do it in private. Let it be for His ears only. Make it your goal to be a woman of *discretion,* not dissension.

Cultivate Gratitude

One of the greatest ways to excel at being gracious and forgiving is to develop a heart of gratitude. In fact, gratitude is one of the best antidotes for depression, anger, and self-pity. Scripture says, "Do all things without complaining and disputing, that you may become blameless and harmless, children of God without fault in the midst of a crooked and perverse generation, among whom you shine as lights in the world" (Philippians 2:14-15). And yet, how many of us think nothing of griping and complaining when things don't turn out exactly as we want?

As Americans, we've been trained to "demand our rights." The message "Get what you deserve! Fight for what you want!" Have it your way!" is all around us. And all too often, we fall for it. We believe we are entitled to comforts, security, money, popularity, and happiness, all the while forgetting we are utterly undeserving of even the very *least* of God's amazing blessings. Instead of being flooded with gratitude for everything He's done for us, we become sullen, depressed, or demanding when any of our "rights" are threatened. We are all too much like the nine healed lepers who never returned to give thanks to God:

> When He saw [the lepers] He said to them, "Go, show yourselves to the priests." And so it was that as they went, they were cleansed. And one of them, when he saw that he was healed, returned, and with a loud voice glorified God, and fell down on his face at His feet, giving Him thanks. And he was a Samaritan. So Jesus answered and said, "Were there not ten cleansed? But where are the nine? Were there not any found who returned to give glory to God except this foreigner?" (Luke 17:14-18).

Like the nine ungrateful lepers, we take the benefits and blessings of Christ and then go our way, entirely forgetting that everything we have comes from Him, that we deserve nothing but death, yet He has given us life.

We must live each day in light of the cross. When we remember the unfathomable sacrifice our heroic Lord has made for us, we are far less apt to gripe, complain, whine, and demand. Rather, we live in humble awe of the incredible gift of what He has done. We shine with gratitude and thanks. We radiate with the beauty and jubilance of a woman who's been given a second chance at life. Petty gripes and complaints no longer seem important in light of His immeasurable gift to us.

Next time you are feeling angry or depressed, try this little experiment. Go away to a quiet place and, with pen and paper ready, begin making a list of all the things in life you are thankful for—all the many ways in which God has blessed you. Enter into a worship time of genuine thanks and praise for all He's given you. Meditate upon the astounding gift of His love and His redemption over your life, even though you were unworthy and undeserving. Soon, your frustration and self-pity will give way to a heart of genuine thanks and gratitude—and a truly grateful woman is a truly beautiful woman!

To cultivate gratitude, we must also remember those who are far less blessed than we are. Recently my friend Annie showed me heart-rending pictures of parents she met in Haiti who were forced to give their children up for adoption in order to save them from the slow, painful death of starvation. Such horrible facts helped put my life into proper perspective. Whenever I started to catch myself inwardly moaning about a financial issue or complaining about the difficulty of raising four children under the age of four, I called to mind those photos. Remembering the heartbroken faces of those Haitian parents quickly put my petty cares to silence. I thanked God for allowing me the amazing gift of raising my children and being able to provide for their needs. I prayed for the Haitian parents—that they would find Jesus Christ and experience His transforming power and provision in their lives. And by God's grace I determined to put all my trivial complaints, gripes, and worries aside.

When Betsy and Corrie first arrived at the German concentration camp, they could scarcely believe how bad the conditions were. Fourteen hundred women had been forced to sleep in a concrete room made to hold only four hundred. The bedding hay was soiled and rancid. Eight putrid, overflowing toilets served the entire room, and to reach them they had to crawl over rows of the overcrowded, sagging platforms that served as the makeshift beds. Shrieks and smothered cries could be heard throughout the room as several of the platforms came crashing down on the women below. The prisoners were exhausted and malnourished, and most did not share a common language. The sound of brawls, screams, slaps, and sobs echoed around the barracks.

The first night Betsy felt a sharp pinch on her leg and then another.

Fleas were ruthlessly attacking. Beside her on the platform, Corrie suddenly bolted up, striking her head against the wood beam overhead. "Betsy!" she hissed. "This place is swarming with fleas! How can we ever survive here?"

"Show us, Lord. Show us how," Betsy prayed aloud. Then she exclaimed, "Corrie! Our Lord has given us the answer! Find that verse in the Bible we read this morning!"

Corrie glanced around quickly to make sure no guards were near. Then she fumbled through the pages of the tiny New Testament they had managed to sneak into the camp with them. In the dim light she squinted and whispered the words. "Rejoice always, pray constantly, give thanks in all circumstances" (1 Thessalonians 5:16-18 RSV).

Betsy's eyes shone. "That's His answer, Corrie! We can give thanks in *all* circumstances! We can start right now to thank Him for every single thing about this new barracks!"

Corrie just stared at Betsy incredulously, and then she looked slowly around the cramped, foul-aired room. "What can there possibly be to give thanks for in *this* place?" she asked skeptically.

Betsy paused, and then smiled again. "Well, being put here together, for one thing." Corrie bit her lip and nodded in surprised agreement.

"And that there was no inspection when we entered—so we were able to keep our Bible," she continued excitedly. "And even for the crowded quarters, so that even more will hear when we are able to share the Scripture with them!" Corrie again nodded thoughtfully.

"Lord, we even thank You for the fleas," Betsy prayed serenely, but Corrie interrupted. "Betsy, there is no way that God can make me grateful for a flea!"

But Betsy was undeterred. Where others saw monstrous, animalistic prison guards, Betsy saw only lonely, wounded souls, desperately in need of her Prince's love. Where others saw hellish, suffocating sleeping quarters, Betsy saw only the opportunity to reach more people with the truth of Jesus Christ. Where others saw fleas, Betsy saw a gift from her Lord. Eventually, it was discovered that their nightly worship services would have been quickly thwarted were it not for the fact that the prison guards refused to enter their disgusting, flea-infested barracks for an inspection. Even the fleas were a miracle from her faithful Lord.[2]

Such a story convicts and inspires me. This is Christlike gratitude at its best.

What circumstances in *your* life can you begin to give thanks for, rather than complain about? Cultivating a heart of gratitude will transform your outlook on life and change you from a fretting, dour, self-focused woman to a peaceful, radiant, Christ-focused one.

Important note: In my book *Set-Apart Femininity,* I talked about certain trials and challenges God does *not* want us to accept and resign ourselves to—attacks from the enemy that often come in the form of discouragement, sickness, spiritual oppression, etc.

We are not to receive these evidences of Satan's work and learn to live with them, but rather rise up in the power of God and wrestle in prayer until the enemy's strongholds are removed from our lives. However, though we are not to accept harassment from the enemy, we can still thank God for the opportunity to learn how to fight, pray, and be strengthened in our faith—just as it says in James 1. All things the enemy means for evil in our lives can be turned to good by His power, and this is something to rejoice in!

Forgive Deep Hurts

Madeline is a young woman with a difficult past. Her father left when she and her sister were young, her mother lived a sordid life of selfish pleasure, and she was abused and betrayed by a cruel man when she was only eighteen. Though she has pretty features, Madeline's eyes are dark and resentful, and her face seems to be locked in a continual scowl. She rarely smiles. She never laughs. The only humor she ever exudes comes in the form of biting sarcasm. Madeline got married a couple of years ago to a nice Christian guy who seemed to want to soothe away her past wounds, but Madeline's extreme bitterness has begun to affect their marriage. She keeps a record of everything her husband does or says that is insensitive. She continually reminds him of his weaknesses and shortcomings. And when he does something hurtful, she refuses to speak to him for days on end.

Madeline's bitterness is not only destroying her marriage, it is destroying her soul. She claims to be a Christian, but she exudes hardness and resentment rather than joy and peace. She holds grudges over the slightest offenses. Her health is suffering as a result of the stress she carries in her inner life. And with each passing year, she grows more and more trapped in her lifestyle of anger and hostility.

Carrie is a young woman with a similar background to Madeline's. Her father was sexually and physically abusive, and her mother was all but absent growing up. She was used and mistreated by several men before she even turned twenty. And she suffered betrayal from friends she deeply trusted.

And yet Carrie's demeanor is completely different than Madeline's. Her face is soft and peaceful. She smiles often. She reaches out to others. She is the kind of friend others can lean on and confide in. Carrie has been set free from bitterness by the power of Jesus Christ. She has leaned upon His strength to forgive those who have so deeply wounded her. She has received the grace to let their offenses go—to learn to love them and see them with compassion, just as Christ does. And as a result, she shines with a beauty others are refreshed by. She is a living testimony of the redemption and power of God.

Whenever we have been deeply wounded, we often feel it is our right to cling to those offenses, to nurse anger and bitterness in our heart toward the guilty person; to see them as a monstrous enemy rather than a person to love and show mercy to. But when we allow a root of bitterness to grow within our heart, as Hebrews says, our inner life becomes distorted and defiled. It's impossible to showcase the beauty of Jesus Christ when we are hosting resentment in our heart. We must let go of our bitterness before it destroys us.

Pursue peace with all people, and holiness, without which no one will see the Lord: looking carefully lest anyone fall short of the grace of God; least any root of bitterness springing up cause trouble, and by this many become defiled (Hebrews 12:14-15).

Do not allow the enemy to gain even more victory from a wound by making room in your heart for bitterness. Take your pain and hurt to Jesus. Lay them at the foot of His cross. Just as Corrie took the hand of her sister's killer in a step of sheer obedience to God, take that first step of letting go of the offense. Trust God to supply the love, mercy, compassion, and grace needed to walk in true forgiveness from this point forward. Sometimes the old feelings might try to creep back in, but when they do, simply call on the name of Jesus and ask Him to cleanse them away from your heart, as far away as the east is from the west. It's a prayer He is always faithful to answer.

Note: If you have struggled with anger toward God for allowing something tragic to happen in your life, I would encourage you to read my book *Set-Apart Femininity*, in which I discuss the common tactic of the enemy to wreak havoc upon our lives and then get us to blame God for it. The book goes into great detail on the work of the enemy in our lives and shows you how to build a wall of spiritual fortification to keep Satan from having unguarded access to your life. It will also help you understand the role of pain and tragedy in your life—and recognize what kind of pain comes from God, and what kind comes from the enemy.

Life is too short to spend it wallowing in bitterness. Even if there are people in your life who seem impossible to forgive, remember that you do not need to accomplish this in your own strength. Everything you need to find complete freedom from resentment and sincere love for those who have hurt you can be found at the foot of the cross. A woman with noble beauty is gracious and forgiving, tenderhearted and compassionate, and she does not keep record of wrongs. If you feel far from such an attitude, ask God to transform you from the inside out. Remember how much He has forgiven you, and ask Him for the grace to show the same mercy toward others.

When you habitually forgive and love instead of resent and hold grudges, you'll glow with a softness and feminine grace that cannot be manufactured any other way.

QUESTIONS AND ANSWERS

Eating Disorders, Physical Flaws,
Body Image Obsession, and More

1. How do I take care of my body without obsessing over it?

Over the years I've heard many Christians translate the concept of "taking care of God's temple" into an excuse for spending all their spare time at the gym or the beauty salon, obsessing over their physical appearance and devoting their best time and energy to improving their "look." But the message of the Gospel is clear—we are not to stroke and coddle self, but die to self. We are not to be consumed with self or our outward appearance; we are to be consumed with Jesus Christ alone. It's simply not possible to be a reflection of the glory of Christ when we are more devoted to worshipping our own bodies than to adoring our King.

American young women are especially vulnerable to getting caught up in the body image rat race. Magazine covers scream at us from checkout counters, urging us to wear the latest clothes and try the latest fad diets. Billboards beckon our attention, hounding us with their impossible standards for feminine allure. Our peers spend their time obsessively dieting and exercising, giving sway to compulsive shopping habits, and preening for hours in front of the mirror. We face daily pressure to worship our bodies and focus our energy on improving them.

Christ said, "Life is more than food, and the body is more than clothing" (Luke 12:23). Do we live as if His words are true? All too many modern girls are consumed with the food they eat (or don't eat) and the clothes they wear (or want to wear.) This is true for women who are caught up in cultural pressures as well as for women who have made it their life's focus to shun society's expectations. I've seen plenty of girls who take great pride in purposely dressing like slobs, never wearing makeup, keeping their hair grungy, and carrying themselves like guys—and I can't help noticing that they are just as enslaved to their image as the girls who spend all their time snatching up the latest trends and looking as sexy as possible.

When it comes to taking care of our body, we should have only one goal—to honor and glorify Jesus Christ. We will not bring glory to His name by exuding the empty charm and sensuality of this world, but neither will we honor Him by treating our body carelessly and sloppily. As set-apart young women, I believe we should treat our body with respect, but not worship or obsession. Here are some ways in which I personally seek to apply this principle in my own life.

I make exercise and eating right a priority. These are not something I stress over, just disciplines I add into my life when possible. I am aware that sometimes God calls us into situations when it is literally impossible to eat well or maintain an exercise schedule of any kind— such as going to a primitive area on the mission field where you are forced to eat exactly as the locals do and where it is dangerous to go out jogging on your own. Being obedient to God is far more important than following a specific formula for health. But whenever I *do* have a choice about eating and exercise, I make it my goal to honor God by disciplining my flesh in these areas.

I'm not talking about following diet and workout programs promoted by the world for the purpose of achieving the right look or ideal weight. Rather, I'm talking about disciplining "my body and making it my slave" as Paul did (1 Corinthians 9:27 NASB) so that I am not a slave to the cravings and whims of my flesh. The less we give our flesh a voice in our life, the more we are able to hear and obey the voice of God's Spirit. If we listen to the cravings of our flesh when it comes to food—especially in a country like America, where we can get virtually any kind of food we want, whenever we want it—we can quickly become the selfish gluttons that the Bible warns against, whose "god is their stomach" (Philippians 3:19 NIV).

Instead of just eating whatever I am craving, I try to eat healthy foods that will build my body up instead of tear it down; foods that will give me strength for the work God has called me to instead of weakening me. I also monitor how *much* I'm eating—again, not as an obsession over my weight, but simply as a discipline to my flesh. In America, it's all too easy to overeat until we are so full we can't take another bite. But this habit is not healthy for our bodies or our spiritual lives. We are not to be servants to our stomachs, but to the Spirit of God. And if He asks us to give up our food for a season so that we can give ourselves to focused prayer, or share our food with someone in need, we need to have enough discipline in this area so that it doesn't seem like an impossible request.

For me, exercising is a great opportunity to conquer laziness. My flesh sometimes balks at the idea of going out for a jog or bike ride, but I've found that when I simply do it anyway, I feel refreshed and invigorated, not to mention stronger for having not listened to the temptation toward lethargy. Often I listen to Scripture or worship music on my iPod as I exercise, which even invigorates me more.

Disciplining my flesh even in small areas like these goes a long way in developing my spiritual stamina, and it also affects the way I feel on a daily basis. Just as dressing like a slob often causes me to feel lethargic toward my tasks and sloppy in my femininity, letting my exercise routine slip and my eating habits become sloppy can have the same effect.

The same is true with clothing, makeup, and other aspects of my physical presentation. If I spend too much time on my personal appearance, it draws attention to myself and not to Christ. But on the flip side, if I spend too *little* time on my appearance, I can become a distraction from His glory as well. I've seen many girls who never seem to wash their hair or take care of their bodies. Their lack of care over their appearance is a distraction to everyone they encounter, and this sends the message that they don't care enough to put any effort into basic grooming. And, of course, I've seen plenty of girls who give so much time to their appearance that they are equally distracting. Our goal should be to make ourselves presentable; remove all distractions; draw attention to our face, eyes, and smile; and let our outward appearance showcase the inner joy, peace, and love Christ is cultivating within our soul.

Here are some questions to ask yourself:

- Do I spend more time on my appearance each day than I do cultivating my relationship with Christ?

- Do I make clothing, dieting, exercising, etc. a higher priority than spiritual growth?

- Do I dress with the goal to gain attention from guys and approval from friends?

- Am I enslaved to fashion trends, dieting, or exercise? (Hint: if you are unwilling to live without these things, that's a sign they have an unhealthy hold on your heart.)

- Do I revere the advice of fashion magazines, clothing commercials, and Hollywood celebrities when it comes to taking care of my body?

If you answered yes to any of these questions, ask God to remake you in this area of your life. Prayerfully consider what steps you might need to take in order to free yourself from the bondage of pop culture body image expectations. For example, stop reading magazines that promote materialism, sensuality, and selfishness. And if going to the mall causes you to become obsessed with your appearance, consider ordering your clothes online or shopping at resale stores instead. Be willing to do whatever it takes to remove unhealthy influences in your life. Remember that your body is meant to be a tool to serve *God's* purposes—not your own selfish agenda. Ask Him to show you how you can bring more glory to His name through your physical appearance.

2. How do I overcome an eating disorder?

This is a very tough issue to speak to because it's often loaded with emotion. Most young women have either struggled with this issue personally or know someone who has. The impossible standards and relentless pressure of our society have escalated women's struggles with eating disorders at an alarming rate. But we must recognize that we are not helpless victims to anorexia and bulimia. Don't just hope that it will go away on its own. An eating disorder is a medical condition and something that needs to be taken seriously. If you are struggling with an eating disorder, I would recommend seeking out godly, biblical counseling and medical help. And I believe it's extremely important to tackle the issue spiritually, not just physically, in order to truly achieve freedom and victory in this area of your life. Here is my take on tackling the spiritual side of the issue.

Eating disorders develop when we start listening to the lies of society and when we attempt to find security and happiness outside of Jesus Christ. When we start believing our body must look a certain way, we can never be fulfilled. An eating disorder is like any other addiction—we must repent of our sin and rely on the transforming power of Jesus Christ to truly set us free from it.

In my book *Authentic Beauty*, I described the subtle way in which sin can overtake our life. It doesn't happen all at once. It starts when we trifle with sin. Whenever we fail to keep vigilant watch over our soul and carelessly expose our hearts and minds to the messages of pop culture, we become vulnerable to making ungodly choices.

When we begin adopting a careless attitude toward the influences of pop culture, participating in its messages and taking its advice, we take the first step down the road to an eating disorder. The moment the temptation comes, and we hear the subtle whisper of the enemy in our ear saying, "You would be so much prettier if you were as skinny as that wraithlike supermodel on the cover of that magazine," we have a choice to make. We can either listen to his voice and entertain his suggestions, or we can immediately choose to tune out the lies and respond with truth: "My life is not my own. I've been bought with a price. I will not look to pop culture's standards to define my security, but to Jesus Christ and the purchase of His cross."

If you have already given in to the sin of starving yourself (or bingeing and purging) in order to gain approval, happiness, or security, then start by confessing it to Christ and asking Him to wash you clean. If the habit of starving yourself has become a controlling addiction in your life, ask Him to set you free by His transforming power. Ask Him to give you grace to turn and walk a different path, starting today. Godly teammates, counselors, medical professionals, and accountability partners can be very helpful as you seek to change your attitudes and patterns. But remember that it is only the power of Jesus Christ that can truly set you free and make you new. He will not only give you freedom from this addiction in your life, but the ability to find your security and fulfillment in Him alone. A great resource for eating disorders is *www.starvingsoul.org*.

3. How do I deal with intense insecurity over my physical flaws?

A woman who is deeply, passionately, intimately in love Jesus Christ glows with a radiance that overpowers even the most noticeable flaws. I've seen many a godly woman light up an entire room with her presence. To study her closely, you would not think of her as beautiful; in fact, she might even have major physical blemishes that would normally be distracting. But when a woman's passion for Jesus Christ is so deep that it is the focal point of her existence, it effervesces from every corner of her being—and she glows with heavenly beauty. No matter what her physical flaws might be, they are unnoticed when Jesus Christ is center stage in her life.

Our Korean daughter, Harper, was born without any fingers. Her sweet little hands look like tiny mittens with only the thumbs sticking out. Since she is only two, she has no concept of feeling strange or insecure about her hands. To her, they are totally normal. Harper is so childlike and free in the way she interacts with others—she is totally devoid of shyness or insecurity. And as a result, most people hardly notice her lack of fingers. They see her cute smile, her chubby cheeks, and the mischievous sparkle in her eyes. It's her complete *lack* of focus on her deformity that makes other people forget about it.

Insecurity is simply an unhealthy focus on yourself rather than a healthy focus on Jesus Christ. It's something the enemy can easily use to keep us turned inward rather than outward. Just like the temptation toward any sin, we must nip thoughts of insecurity in the bud the moment they begin to arise. As soon as the enemy comes in with whispers of, "Everyone is noticing your physical shortcomings. There is nothing attractive about you—no one wants to be around you," your response must be immediate. Instead of entertaining those thoughts and meditating upon them, fight back with truth, Scripture, and prayer. Remind the enemy (and yourself) that you have been created in the image of God, that your life has been redeemed by the blood of Christ, and that you are precious in His sight. Remember that Christ loved you so much He gave His very life to rescue you. And your calling as a daughter of the King is not to wallow in selfishness and insecurity, but to joyfully turn outward and share His amazing love with others.

If you begin to ignore thoughts of insecurity and deliberately choose to smile, reach out to others, and focus on being an example of Christ, you will soon realize that insecurity has no soil in which to grow. It may take some time before this principle becomes a habit in your life, but if you lean on the grace and strength of God, He will give you all that you need to triumph in this area.

If you have a major physical distraction that you can do something about, then prayerfully consider doing so. There is nothing more spiritual about keeping your teeth crooked when braces could straighten them, or leaving a huge wart on the end of your nose when a doctor could easily remove it. If you are overweight and constantly preoccupied with thoughts about it, ask God to give you the discipline and focus to take charge of your eating habits. Removing distractions can help remove the temptation to worry about them and obsess over them. Just remember not to put off shining with Christlike confidence until your flaws have been dealt with. Beware of saying, "I'll finally be happy when I lose weight" or "I'll turn outward once I get my nose fixed." Our security must come from Him, not primarily from the removal of a physical distraction.

St. Francis of Assis said:

> Lord grant me the serenity to accept the things I cannot change, the courage to change the things I can, and the wisdom to know the difference.

That's a great rule of thumb when it comes to dealing with physical flaws. Our sense of strength and security must come from Christ alone. We must trust Him for the ability to accept what we cannot (or should not) change in our appearance, the courage to change what needs to be changed, and the wisdom to know the difference.

4. I don't think I'm very good looking, and guys never seem attracted to me. Is there any hope that a guy will one day find me beautiful?

Psalm 45 gives a vivid depiction of the kind of feminine beauty that captivates the heart of a noble warrior. Verse 13 says, "The king's daughter is all glorious within" (NASB). "Within" literally means "inward" or "inner part." It is the glorious radiance of her *inner life* that makes the king's daughter so lovely and desirable. A godly man who has been transformed by the life of Christ will first and foremost be attracted to your *heart,* not your physical appearance. It will be the beauty of Christ shining through you that wins his affection. In the eyes of the man God has chosen for you (if His plan for you is marriage), you will be radiant with a beauty that does not fade with time.

I recently read the inspiring true story of how C.T. Studd (a missionary to China in the late 1800s) met his wife. He wrote,

> She spoke to me—I do not say with her eyes, not her tongue—she was keeping that in reserve—she spoke with her acts. I did not marry her for her pretty face; I married her for her handsome actions towards the Lord Jesus Christ and those He sent her to save. In fact, I can well remember the afternoon when I was sitting, talking to a missionary in Taiyuen, and he twitted me on being engaged to the prettiest girl in all Shanghai. Now that, I tell you in all truth, was an absolute shock to me, for certainly I had never thought of her pretty face. In fact, until this day I verily believe that of all God's many good gifts, the least of all is good looks.[1]

Physical attraction is certainly a fun and healthy part of a God-scripted love story, but it's merely meant to be an outflow of a much deeper attraction—two hearts dazzled by the beauty of Christ they see flowing from each other's hearts. The world continually screams at us about the importance of being outwardly beautiful in order to find true love. But in God's economy, "charm is deceitful and beauty is passing, but a woman who fears the LORD, she shall be praised" (Proverbs 31:30).

The more you build your life around Jesus Christ and make Him the centerpiece of your existence, the more you will radiate with the kind of beauty that will not only turn a godly man's head, but his heart.

FINAL THOUGHTS

Beauty in a Nutshell

In 1880, Christina Rosetti wrote these words:

> *How beautiful are the arms which have embraced Christ,*
> *the hands which have touched Christ, the eyes which*
> *have gazed upon Christ, the lips which have spoken*
> *with Christ, the feet which have followed Christ. How*
> *beautiful are the hands which have worked the works of*
> *Christ, the feet which treading in His footsteps have gone*
> *about doing good, the lips which have spread abroad His*
> *Name, the lives which have been counted loss for Him.*
>
> —CHRISTINA ROSETTI

There is no other path to lasting beauty. There is no other way a woman can radiate with the sparkle of her King. To effervesce with captivating loveliness, we must be overtaken by the Author of all true beauty. We must exchange our ugliness for His royal splendor.

We must live a life of daily passionate intimacy with Him and become His hands and feet to this lost and dying world.

Mary Slessor, a young Scottish missionary who spent more than 30 years serving the natives of Africa, sacrificed her physical beauty in order to pour her life out for the least. She lived among the poorest of the poor, in a mud hut with no comforts or conveniences. She toiled daily in the hot sun, helping the filthy, the diseased, and the dying, whom no one else was willing to touch. A reporter who came to Africa to do a story on her encountered a woman with shabby clothes, weathered skin, and hands calloused and rough from hard labor. And yet, he wrote, there was something about this woman. Something different. Something beautiful. Her quiet peace, the joy in her eyes, the sparkle in her smile, and her unmatched courage made her stand out among all other women he'd ever seen. "She conquered me," he said. Mary was a true lily among thorns.[1]

True beauty does not depend upon clothes, makeup, or malls. It does not come from perfect skin or an ideal figure. It's not found in the advice of modern magazines. It can't be seen in the glitz and glamour of Hollywood.

True beauty, in a nutshell, is found in a soul completely surrendered to Jesus Christ, a heart consumed by Him alone, and a life eagerly poured out for His sake. That is when we will sparkle with heaven's radiance and stand out from among all other women like a lily among thorns (Song of Solomon 2:2).

Spurgeon's words capture it perfectly:

> The lily among thorns...has incomparable beauty...When I think of Christ's lilies, adorned in His own righteousness and bearing His own image, I feel that I may repeat my Master's words and say with emphasis, "Solomon in all his glory was not arrayed like one of these!" In Christ's esteem, His Church bears the bell for beauty. She is the fairest among women...if you take worldlings at their best and in their

bravest attire—in their pomp and glory and parade—they are but as thorns in contrast with His Church…The thorns are worthless. They flourish and spread and cumber the ground, but they yield no fruit and only grow to be cut down for the oven…As for the lily, it is a thing of beauty and a joy forever. It lives shedding sweet perfume and when it is gathered, its loveliness adorns the chamber to which it is taken. So does the true saint bless his generation while here and when he is taken away he is regarded even in Heaven above as one of the flowers of God![2]

Precious sisters, by the grace of God may we become the beautiful lilies God has called us to be. Starting today, may we shed abroad the sweet perfume of our Prince through every pore of our existence.

NOTES

Chapter 1—The Vision

1. Edith Deen, *Great Women of the Christian Faith* (Westwood, NJ: Barbour, 1959), 243.
2. Ibid., 226.
3. Ibid., 205.
4. Elisabeth Dodds, *Marriage to a Difficult Man* (Louisville, KY: Westminister John Knox Press, 1971), 17.
5. C.H. Spurgeon, "The Lily Among Thorns," sermon #1525, spurgeongems.org.

Chapter 2—Selfless Beauty

1. Wendy Shalit, *A Return to Modesty* (New York, NY: Touchstone, 2000), 2.
2. Oswald Chambers, *The Complete Works of Oswald Chambers* (Grand Rapids, MI: Discovery House Publishers, 2000), 711.
3. Amy Carmichael, *Gold Cord (Fort Washington, PA: CLC Publications, 1991)*, 177-78.
4. Jackie Pullinger, "God Uses the Foolish Things," audio sermon on www.sermonindex .net.
5. Ian Thomas, *The Mystery of Godliness* (Grand Rapids, MI: Zondervan,1964), 185.

Chapter 4—Excelling in Manners

1. Corrie ten Boom, *Tramp for the Lord* (Fort Washington, PA: Christian Literature Crusade, 2008), 17, 24.

Chapter 6—Dressing with Selfless Style

1. Christa Taylor, personal interview, used by permission.
2. Edith Deen, *Great Women of the Christian Faith,* 221.
3. Amy Carmichael, *Gold Cord* (London, England: London Society for Promoting Christian Knowledge, 1947), 15.
4. Edith Deen, *Great Women of the Christian Faith,* 243.
5. Elisabeth Elliot, *A Chance to Die: The Life and Legacy of Amy Carmichael* (Grand Rapids, MI: Revel, 1987), 73.

Chapter 7—Sacred Beauty

1. Wendy Shalit, *A Return to Modesty,* 174.
2. Amy Carmichael, from the poem, "Divine Paradox," published in *Mountain Breezes: The Collected Poems of Amy Carmichael* (Fort Washington, PA: CLC Publications, 1999), 174. Used by permission. All rights reserved.

Chapter 8—The Secrets of Sacred Living

1. Corrie ten Boom, John and Elizabeth Sherrill, *The Hiding Place* (Uhrichsville, OH: Barbour and Company, Inc., 1971), 150.
2. Thomas Kinkade, *Simpler Times* (Eugene, OR: Harvest House, 1996), 13-17.

Chapter 9—Excelling at the Sacred Art of Hospitality

1. Amy Carmichael, *If* (Fort Washington, PA: Christian Literature Crusade, 2001), 17, 33, 45, 60.

Chapter 10—Awakening to the Romance of Life

Epigraph: Thomas Kinkade, *Simpler Times,* 76-77.

Chapter 11—Noble Beauty

1. Corrie ten Boom, *Tramp for the Lord* (New York, NY: Penguin Group, 1978), 55.
2. Corrie ten Boom, *The Hiding Place,* 180-84.

Questions and Answers

1. Norman P. Grubb, *C.T. Studd, Cricketer & Pioneer* (Fort Washington, PA: Christian Literature Crusade, 1933), 75.

Final Thoughts

1. Deen, *Great Women of the Christian Faith,* 284.
2. C.H. Spurgeon, "The Lily Among Thorns," sermon #1525, spurgeongems.org.

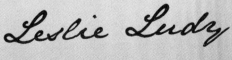

Take the message deeper:

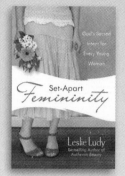

SET-APART FEMININITY

Do you long for something more than the shallow, self-focused, pleasure-seeking femininity so prevalent today? Do you want a focus beyond chasing male approval and pop culture appeal? Do you need a fresh vision of God's amazing purpose for your life as a young woman? Are you ready to become one of the few in this generation who will make an eternal impact upon this world?

Discover *Set-Apart Femininity.* This is a powerful, candid, conversational book in which Leslie Ludy passes on a compelling vision for femininity that can forever alter your existence and take you far beyond the unfulfilling trends of modern culture. This book is not the same old mediocre message you've always heard. It's a radical call to a counter-culture lifestyle in which every aspect of your femininity—from the way you relate with guys to the focus and direction of your life—is shaped by an intimate relationship with the King of kings. It's the kind of heroic femininity that the world-changing women of history understood. And it's well within your grasp, no matter where you've been.

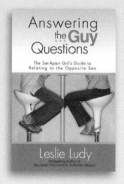

ANSWERING THE GUY QUESTIONS

Answering the Guy Questions tackles some of the toughest questions Leslie gets asked about guy/girl relationships. It is very specific and practical and helps you apply the set-apart lifestyle to the often-confusing area of guys. It also addresses the issue of modern male mediocrity—it will give you a vision for how you can help the guys in your life experience true manhood as God intended it to be, in all of its glory, strength, nobility, and honor. If you have ever been discouraged, disgusted, depressed, or even defeated by the state of modern guys, this book can infuse you with vision, hope, and a practical means of doing something about it! As an added bonus, this book is short and to the point—a very easy read if you don't have a lot of time.

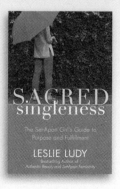

SACRED SINGLENESS

Are you single? Do you struggle with discontentment, impatience, and the constant pressures of pop culture? In this powerful and refreshing book, Leslie introduces you to God's pattern for sacred, purpose-filled, world-changing singleness. She invites you to discover a passionate romance with the ultimate Bridegroom—a romance that will satisfy the deepest desires of your soul, whether you are married or single. *Sacred Singleness* will show you how to let God script your love story in His own time and way, overcome loneliness and jealousy toward friends getting married, triumph over the temptation to settle for less than God's best, enjoy a fulfilling life before you meet your husband, and handle the fear of being single for life.

To learn more about Harvest House books and
to read sample chapters, log on to our website:

www.harvesthousepublishers.com

HARVEST HOUSE PUBLISHERS
EUGENE, OREGON